Table of content

Page 1 .... Why that book?

Page 4   Chapter 1
Page 3 .... Airbnb Hosting
Page 5 ....Overview of Airbnb & the opportunity it presents for hosts
Page 7 ....A Traveler's Perspective on the World of Hosting
Page 9 ....The importance of standout listings in a crowded marketplace
Page 11 ....Setting the right expectations for the reader

Page 13   Chapter 2
Page 14 ....Understanding Airbnb's Algorithm
Page 16 ...How Airbnb's search algorithm works & factors that affect listing visibility
Page 18 ....Tips for improving your listing's search ranking

Page 20   Chapter 3
Page 21 ....Crafting the Perfect Listing
Page 22 ....The best guidance on writing compelling titles and descriptions
Page 24 ....Titles examples
Page 26 ....The importance of honesty & transparency in your listing details

Page 28   Chapter 4
Page 29 ....Professional Photography Tips
Page 31 ....Why high-quality photos are crucial for your listing
Page 33 ....DIY photography tips for hosts
Page 35 ....When to consider hiring a professional photographer
Page 37 ....How to Take Great Airbnb Photos
Page 38 ....Optimal Number of Photos & Airbnb's Recommendations
Page 39 ....Essential Equipment for Capturing Your Airbnb
Page 41 ....9 Helpful Hints for Perfect Airbnb Photography

Page 43   Chapter 5
Page 44 ....Pricing Strategies for Maximum Profit
Page 46 ....Understanding your market & competitive pricing
Page 48 ....Dynamic pricing tools & how to use them
Page 49 ....Seasonal pricing adjustments & special offers

Page 51   Chapter 6
Page 52 ....Enhancing Guest Experience
Page 54 ....Tips for creating a welcoming & memorable stay
Page 56 ....The importance of amenities & personal touches
Page 58 ....Handling guest communications effectively

Table of content

Page 60   Chapter 7
Page 63 ....Managing Reviews & Feedback
Page 65 ....Strategies for encouraging positive reviews
Page 65 ....How to respond to reviews, both positive and negative
Page 67 ....Using feedback to improve your listing & guest experience

Page 69   Chapter 8
Page 70 ....Marketing Your Airbnb
Page 72 ...Beyond the platform: Marketing your listing on social media & other channels
Page 74 ....Building a brand for your Airbnb rental
Page 76 ....Partnering Locally to Elevate Guest Experiences

Page 78   Chapter 9
Page 79 ....Legal Considerations & Best Practices
Page 81 ....Navigating local regulations & Airbnb policies
Page 83 ....Insurance & safety tips for hosts
Page 85 ....Ethical hosting practices

Page 87   Chapter 10
Page 88 ....Scaling Your Airbnb Business
Page 90 ....Expanding your portfolio with additional properties
Page 92 ....Outsourcing and automating tasks for efficiency
Page 94 ....Long-term strategies for success in the Airbnb market

Page 96   Conclusion: Mastering the Art of Airbnb Hosting

Why that book?

Welcome to Your Airbnb Superhost Transformation!

Step into a world where your Airbnb listing isn't just a place to stay, it's an experience. My name is Mario L. Gagnon, and I'm here to be your enthusiastic guide on this journey to transform your hosting experience.

My passion for travel ignited a fire within me. Backpacking through Central America, I wasn't just a tourist, I was a guest – a discerning one, searching for that perfect stay that would elevate my exploration. Each unique accommodation, from charming hostels to luxurious eco-lodges, became a masterclass in hospitality. I soaked in the details, the thoughtful touches, the way a space could truly resonate with a traveler.

But there was a flip side to the coin. I also encountered listings with untapped potential. Places with hidden gems – a breathtaking view, a cozy reading nook, a story waiting to be told – yet they struggled to capture the hearts (and clicks) of potential guests. It was a disconnect that fueled my desire to bridge the gap.

This book is the culmination of that desire. It's where my expertise in digital and AI marketing, honed through years of professional success, merges with the soul of a passionate traveler. You see, in today's digital age, simply listing your property isn't enough. Success lies in mastering the art of online marketing, understanding what makes travelers tick, and leveraging the power of AI to create a listing that pops off the screen.

Here's a taste of what awaits you on this transformative journey:

- **Crafting an irresistible listing:** We'll delve into the psychology of guest attraction, helping you write captivating descriptions, showcase your space with stunning photography, and craft headlines that compel clicks.
- **The power of AI marketing:** We'll explore how AI tools can optimize your listing, target the right audience, and personalize your guest experience. No more guesswork, just data-driven strategies for maximum impact.
- **Unlocking guest behavior:** We'll peel back the layers of what truly motivates travelers, helping you anticipate their needs and create a space that feels like a home away from home.
- **From novice to Superhost:** Whether you're just starting out or looking to refine your existing listing, this book offers a clear roadmap to success.
- **The secrets of a thriving Airbnb host:** We'll touch upon everything from revenue management strategies to fostering positive guest reviews and building a loyal following.

This isn't just a book, it's your key to unlocking the full potential of your Airbnb listing. By the end of this journey, you'll be armed with the knowledge and tools to not only become a master Airbnb host but also create a space that fosters unforgettable memories for your guests and a rewarding experience for yourself.

So, are you ready to dive in? Let's unlock the secrets to becoming a digital-era Airbnb Superhost!

Chapter 1
Airbnb Hosting

Chapter 1

Airbnb Hosting

As we embark on this journey together through the world of Airbnb hosting, I want to start by sharing a fundamental truth that has guided me throughout my own hosting experience: the essence of being a successful Airbnb host lies in attentiveness, responsiveness, and presence. As someone deeply immersed in the nuances of digital and AI marketing, I've learned that these principles are not just applicable to the digital world but are crucial in the realm of hospitality and accommodation.

Being attentive to your guests starts long before they step through your door. It begins the moment they land on your listing. Every question, every inquiry they have, is an opportunity for you to demonstrate your commitment to their needs and comfort. This attentiveness is what sets apart a good host from a great one. It's about understanding not just the explicit requests they make but also anticipating their unspoken needs. Whether it's providing detailed guides to local attractions or ensuring your space caters to the little comforts of home, your attentiveness speaks volumes.

Responsiveness, on the other hand, is your currency in the fast-paced world of Airbnb hosting. In a digital age where information is at our fingertips, guests expect quick and clear communication. Whether it's a question about your property's amenities or a request for an early check-in, your ability to respond swiftly not only enhances your guests' experience but also boosts your reputation on the platform. Remember, every interaction is a chance to impress and a step towards becoming a top-rated host.

Lastly, being present for your guests when they need something cannot be overstated. While it's not always possible to be physically present, especially for those managing properties remotely, presence can also mean being readily available or having systems in place to address any issues promptly. It's about ensuring your guests feel supported throughout their stay, knowing that their host is just a message away should they need anything.

As we delve deeper into the intricacies of Airbnb hosting in the following pages, keep these principles in mind. Attentiveness, responsiveness, and presence are not just strategies; they are the foundation upon which memorable guest experiences are built. They are what will differentiate your listing in a crowded marketplace and pave the way for your success as an Airbnb host. Join me as we explore how to apply these principles effectively, ensuring that every guest who stays with you leaves with a story worth sharing.

Chapter 1-1

Overview of Airbnb & the opportunity it presents for hosts.

In the landscape of travel and accommodation, Airbnb has emerged as a transformative platform, not just for travelers seeking unique and personal experiences but for hosts looking to tap into a lucrative market. As we embark on this first chapter, I extend a warm welcome to those of you who are new to the Airbnb hosting community. Before diving into the intricacies of creating and promoting your listing, it's crucial to grasp the vast opportunities that Airbnb offers and understand the landscape you're about to enter.

Airbnb has democratized travel accommodation, allowing anyone with a spare room, apartment, or entire house to become a host. This platform provides a unique opportunity to monetize your property, but more than that, it offers a chance to meet people from all walks of life and share your local culture and hospitality. For those new to the business, understanding the potential of Airbnb is the first step towards building a successful hosting experience.

The opportunity for hosts on Airbnb extends beyond mere financial gains. It's about creating a space that feels like home for travelers, offering them a more personal and authentic experience than traditional hotels can provide. This personal touch not only leads to higher guest satisfaction but also to repeat bookings and positive reviews, which are gold in the Airbnb ecosystem.

However, the opportunity comes with its challenges. The market is competitive, with millions of listings worldwide. Standing out requires more than just listing your space; it involves strategic marketing, exceptional guest communication, and a commitment to providing a stellar experience. For newcomers, this might seem daunting, but with the right approach and mindset, it's entirely achievable.

Chapter 1-1

If you're new to the Airbnb business, this section is your starting point. Here, we'll cover the foundational aspects of becoming an Airbnb host, from understanding the platform's policies and how to set up your listing to mastering the art of guest relations. This book aims to equip you with the knowledge and tools needed to navigate the Airbnb marketplace confidently. Remember, every successful Airbnb host started exactly where you are now—curious and eager to learn. The journey from listing your space to becoming a sought-after host is a learning curve, but with dedication and the insights shared in this book, you're well on your way to unlocking the full potential of your property. Airbnb hosting is not just a business; it's an adventure in hospitality, cultural exchange, and personal growth. Let's embark on this journey together, transforming your space into a welcoming haven for travelers and a profitable venture for you.

Chapter 1-2

A Traveler's Perspective on the World of Hosting

Reflecting on my extensive travels, where I've had the privilege of staying in over 100 Airbnb properties across various destinations, I've gained a unique perspective on the transformative power of this platform. As someone who spends nearly 80 days a year in different Airbnbs, I've witnessed firsthand the incredible opportunities it presents for hosts and the unparalleled experiences it offers to guests like myself. Airbnb has undeniably revolutionized the way we explore the world, providing a more personalized, comfortable, and authentic travel experience compared to traditional accommodations.

One of the most striking aspects of using Airbnb is the diversity of accommodations available, catering to every possible preference and need. Whether it's a cozy apartment in the heart of the city, a serene getaway in the countryside, or something as unique as a treehouse or a castle, Airbnb has made these experiences accessible to travelers around the globe. This variety not only enriches the travel experience but also opens up new possibilities for hosts to share their unique spaces with an international audience.

For hosts, the opportunity to showcase their property and local area is immense. Through my travels, I've been fortunate to encounter hosts who truly embody the spirit of hospitality, going above and beyond to ensure a memorable stay. These hosts have introduced me to the local culture, cuisine, and hidden gems of their communities, making each visit unforgettable. It's clear that Airbnb provides a platform for hosts to not just rent out their space but to act as ambassadors for their region, fostering a deeper connection between guests and the places they visit.

The flexibility and personal touch offered by Airbnb are unparalleled. As a guest, the ability to select accommodations that meet my specific needs and preferences has been a game-changer. From the amenities offered to the location's convenience, Airbnb allows for a tailored travel experience that traditional hotels often cannot match. Moreover, the personal interactions with hosts add a layer of warmth and authenticity to the travel experience, something that has become increasingly important to me and many other travelers.

Chapter 1-2

Financially, Airbnb offers competitive pricing options that cater to a wide range of budgets, making travel more accessible to a broader audience. For hosts, this translates into a lucrative opportunity to monetize their properties and invest in their passions or projects. The economic impact of Airbnb on local communities is also significant, as it drives tourism and supports local businesses, contributing to the overall vibrancy and sustainability of the areas where it operates.

In my journey as an Airbnb guest, the platform has not only facilitated my adventures but has also enriched them with genuine human connections, cultural exchanges, and the comfort of feeling at home, no matter where in the world I am. The opportunity Airbnb presents for hosts to share their world with travelers like me is truly remarkable, offering a win-win scenario that enhances the travel experience while providing a sustainable income source.

As I look forward to my future travels, I'm excited about the new experiences that await, the people I'll meet, and the homes that will briefly become my own. Airbnb has undoubtedly transformed the landscape of travel, and I'm grateful for the doors it has opened for both guests and hosts alike.

Chapter 1-3

The importance of standout listings in a crowded marketplace

In the bustling world of Airbnb, where millions of listings vie for the attention of travelers, the importance of creating a standout listing cannot be overstated. As we delve into this crucial aspect of Airbnb hosting, I want to emphasize to both new and seasoned hosts alike the transformative power of a well-crafted listing. In a marketplace as crowded and diverse as Airbnb, your listing is not just a space for rent; it's your personal brand, your invitation to the world, and most importantly, your key to success.

A standout listing does more than just attract guests; it captivates, persuades, and creates an immediate sense of belonging. In today's digital age, where the average attention span is shorter than ever, making a strong first impression is critical. Your listing must not only be visible but also memorable. This means going beyond the basics of clear photos and accurate descriptions. It involves storytelling, where every element of your listing - from the title to the amenities you highlight - weaves together a compelling narrative about the unique experience awaiting your guests.

The competition on Airbnb is fierce, but it's also an opportunity to differentiate yourself. Think about what makes your property unique. Is it the breathtaking view from the balcony? The cozy, art-filled interior? Or perhaps it's your unparalleled hospitality and local knowledge. Identifying and showcasing these unique selling points (USPs) can elevate your listing from ordinary to extraordinary.

Moreover, in a crowded marketplace, optimization is key. Understanding and leveraging Airbnb's search algorithm can significantly increase your listing's visibility. Factors such as response rate, review scores, and the completeness of your listing all play a role in where you appear in search results. But visibility is just the first step; converting views into bookings requires that your listing resonates with potential guests on a personal level.

For those new to the Airbnb business, crafting a standout listing might seem like a daunting task. However, it's a critical investment in your hosting journey. A standout listing not only attracts more guests but also sets the stage for positive reviews and repeat bookings, creating a virtuous cycle that can sustain and grow your Airbnb business.

Chapter 1-3

In this chapter, we will explore the strategies and insights necessary to create a listing that not only stands out but also stands the test of time. From photography tips and writing compelling descriptions to optimizing your listing for search and leveraging guest feedback, every piece of advice is aimed at helping you carve out your niche in the Airbnb marketplace.

Remember, the goal is not just to list your space but to tell a story that invites guests into your world. With the right approach, your listing can transcend the ordinary, turning curious browsers into eager guests and contributing to a thriving, sustainable hosting experience. Let's embark on this journey together, transforming your listing into a beacon that shines brightly in the crowded marketplace of Airbnb.

Chapter 1-4

Setting the right expectations for the reader

In the bustling world of Airbnb, where millions of listings vie for the attention of travelers, the importance of creating a standout listing cannot be overstated. As we delve into this crucial aspect of Airbnb hosting, I want to emphasize to both new and seasoned hosts alike the transformative power of a well-crafted listing. In a marketplace as crowded and diverse as Airbnb, your listing is not just a space for rent; it's your personal brand, your invitation to the world, and most importantly, your key to success.

A standout listing does more than just attract guests; it captivates, persuades, and creates an immediate sense of belonging. In today's digital age, where the average attention span is shorter than ever, making a strong first impression is critical. Your listing must not only be visible but also memorable. This means going beyond the basics of clear photos and accurate descriptions. It involves storytelling, where every element of your listing - from the title to the amenities you highlight - weaves together a compelling narrative about the unique experience awaiting your guests.

The competition on Airbnb is fierce, but it's also an opportunity to differentiate yourself. Think about what makes your property unique. Is it the breathtaking view from the balcony? The cozy, art-filled interior? Or perhaps it's your unparalleled hospitality and local knowledge. Identifying and showcasing these unique selling points (USPs) can elevate your listing from ordinary to extraordinary.

Moreover, in a crowded marketplace, optimization is key. Understanding and leveraging Airbnb's search algorithm can significantly increase your listing's visibility. Factors such as response rate, review scores, and the completeness of your listing all play a role in where you appear in search results. But visibility is just the first step; converting views into bookings requires that your listing resonates with potential guests on a personal level.

For those new to the Airbnb business, crafting a standout listing might seem like a daunting task. However, it's a critical investment in your hosting journey. A standout listing not only attracts more guests but also sets the stage for positive reviews and repeat bookings, creating a virtuous cycle that can sustain and grow your Airbnb business.

Chapter 1-4

In this chapter, we will explore the strategies and insights necessary to create a listing that not only stands out but also stands the test of time. From photography tips and writing compelling descriptions to optimizing your listing for search and leveraging guest feedback, every piece of advice is aimed at helping you carve out your niche in the Airbnb marketplace.

Remember, the goal is not just to list your space but to tell a story that invites guests into your world. With the right approach, your listing can transcend the ordinary, turning curious browsers into eager guests and contributing to a thriving, sustainable hosting experience. Let's embark on this journey together, transforming your listing into a beacon that shines brightly in the crowded marketplace of Airbnb.

Chapter 2
Understanding Airbnb's Algorithm

Chapter 2

Understanding Airbnb's Algorithm

As we venture deeper into the realm of successful Airbnb hosting, a critical component emerges that often remains shrouded in mystery for many: Airbnb's search algorithm. This chapter is dedicated to demystifying this crucial aspect, guiding you through the intricacies of how Airbnb's platform operates behind the scenes to match guests with their ideal accommodations. Understanding this algorithm is not just about gaining technical knowledge; it's about aligning your hosting practices with the platform's mechanics to enhance your listing's visibility and attractiveness to potential guests.

Airbnb's search algorithm is a dynamic and sophisticated system designed to provide the best possible matches between hosts and guests. At its core, the algorithm aims to create a win-win situation: guests find their perfect stay, and hosts increase their bookings. However, to leverage this system to your advantage, it's essential to grasp the factors that influence your listing's ranking within search results. These factors include but are not limited to, the completeness of your listing, the quality and recency of reviews, response rates, and the overall guest experience you provide.

For many hosts, particularly those new to the platform, the algorithm can seem like an insurmountable barrier to success. However, with the right approach, it becomes a powerful tool in your arsenal. This chapter will break down the key components of the algorithm, offering practical tips and strategies to optimize your listing. From understanding the importance of a complete and compelling profile to mastering the art of prompt and effective communication with guests, every piece of advice is aimed at boosting your visibility on Airbnb.

Moreover, we'll explore the significance of pricing strategies, availability settings, and the impact of instant bookings on your search ranking. The goal is to provide you with a comprehensive understanding of how Airbnb's algorithm works and how you can make it work for you. By the end of this chapter, you'll be equipped with the knowledge to make informed decisions about managing your listing, ensuring it reaches its full potential in attracting guests.

Chapter 2

As we delve into the complexities of Airbnb's search algorithm, remember that the ultimate aim is to enhance the guest experience. The algorithm favors listings that not only meet but exceed guest expectations. Therefore, aligning your hosting practices with these principles not only improves your standing within the algorithm but also contributes to a more successful, rewarding hosting experience.

Understanding Airbnb's algorithm is akin to unlocking a secret language of success on the platform. It empowers you to make strategic decisions that elevate your listing, ensuring it stands out in a sea of options. Let's embark on this journey of discovery together, transforming your approach to Airbnb hosting and setting the stage for increased bookings, satisfied guests, and a thriving rental business.

Chapter 2-1

How Airbnb's search algorithm works & factors that affect listing visibility

Understanding how Airbnb's search algorithm works is akin to unlocking a treasure chest for any host aiming to maximize their listing's visibility and attract more guests. This sophisticated system is designed to match guests with the perfect accommodations for their needs, but it also serves as a competitive arena for hosts. To navigate this landscape successfully, it's crucial to comprehend the factors that influence your listing's position in search results. Let's delve into the mechanics of Airbnb's search algorithm and explore the key elements that affect your listing's visibility.

1. Completeness and Quality of Your Listing

Airbnb rewards listings that provide a comprehensive and high-quality experience for potential guests. This means having a complete profile, detailed descriptions, high-resolution photos, and all amenities listed. The algorithm favors listings that offer guests a clear and thorough understanding of what they can expect, reducing the likelihood of mismatches and enhancing guest satisfaction.

2. Guest Reviews and Ratings

Feedback from past guests plays a pivotal role in your listing's search ranking. High ratings and positive reviews signal to Airbnb that your property offers a superior guest experience, prompting the algorithm to rank it higher. Conversely, negative feedback can significantly impact your visibility. Engaging with reviews, both positive and negative, demonstrates your commitment to guest satisfaction and can mitigate the effects of less favorable reviews.

3. Response Rate and Speed

Airbnb values hosts who are responsive and communicative. Your response rate and the speed at which you reply to inquiries and booking requests directly influence your search ranking. Quick responses not only improve your visibility but also enhance the guest experience, making potential guests feel valued and supported.

4. Pricing Strategy

Competitive and dynamic pricing can affect your listing's attractiveness and, by extension, its visibility. Airbnb's algorithm considers price competitiveness within your local market. Listings priced appropriately for their features, location, and the current demand are more likely to be shown to potential guests. Utilizing Airbnb's pricing tools can help you adjust your rates in real-time, ensuring your listing remains competitive

5. Booking Frequency and Cancellations

The algorithm favors listings with higher booking rates and fewer cancellations. Frequent bookings signal to Airbnb that guests find your listing appealing, which can lead to higher placement in search results. On the other hand, cancellations, especially those initiated by the host, can negatively impact your listing's visibility.

6. Search Relevance and Guest Preferences

Airbnb's algorithm is designed to deliver personalized search results based on guest preferences and past behavior. This means your listing might rank differently for various users. Factors such as location, price, amenities, and even the language used in your listing can influence its relevance to a specific search query.

7. Seasonality and Market Dynamics

The algorithm adjusts for seasonal trends and local market dynamics, affecting how listings are ranked. Understanding these patterns and adjusting your listing accordingly (e.g., updating your calendar, adjusting prices, or highlighting seasonal amenities) can improve your visibility during peak and off-peak seasons.

In essence, Airbnb's search algorithm is a complex, ever-evolving system that aims to balance guest needs with host offerings. By focusing on the factors outlined above, you can optimize your listing to align with the algorithm's criteria, enhancing your visibility, attracting more guests, and ultimately, achieving greater success on the platform. Remember, the key to mastering Airbnb's search algorithm lies in understanding and strategically addressing these critical elements.

Chapter 2-2

Tips for improving your listing's search ranking

Navigating the intricacies of Airbnb's search algorithm can seem daunting, but understanding how to enhance your listing's search ranking is crucial for maximizing visibility and attracting more guests. As we delve into this topic, I'll share actionable tips that can elevate your listing's position in search results, drawing from my expertise in digital and AI marketing. These strategies are designed not just to game the system but to genuinely improve the guest experience, thereby aligning with Airbnb's ultimate goal.

1. Optimize Your Listing's Completeness

Ensure every section of your listing is filled out in detail. From the description to the amenities, completeness is key. Airbnb's algorithm favors listings that provide a comprehensive snapshot of what guests can expect. This includes high-quality photos (with captions that describe the benefits of each space), a detailed description of your place, and a complete list of amenities. Remember, the more information you provide, the more confident guests will feel in booking your space.

2. Focus on Stellar Guest Experiences

Positive reviews significantly impact your search ranking. Focus on creating memorable stays for your guests by offering clean, comfortable accommodations and adding personal touches that make your space unique. Prompt and friendly communication, clear instructions, and local recommendations can also enhance the guest experience. After each stay, encourage satisfied guests to leave a review; a polite reminder can go a long way.

3. Maintain a High Response Rate and Speed

Being responsive is crucial. Aim to reply to inquiries and booking requests as quickly as possible, ideally within a few hours. Airbnb tracks response times and considers this when determining your listing's search ranking. Setting up instant book can also improve your response rate, as it allows guests to book your listing without waiting for approval, thereby increasing your attractiveness to both guests and the algorithm.

4. Implement a Dynamic Pricing Strategy:

Price competitively by researching similar listings in your area and adjusting your rates based on demand, seasonality, and local events. Utilize Airbnb's pricing tools to stay competitive and consider offering discounts for longer stays or last-minute bookings. A well-thought-out pricing strategy can make your listing more appealing to potential guests and improve your search visibility.

5. Update Your Calendar Regularly

A frequently updated calendar is a signal to Airbnb's algorithm that your listing is active and reliable. Regular updates can improve your search ranking, as it assures the platform that your availability is accurate, reducing the risk of double bookings or cancellations.

6. Leverage Keywords in Your Listing

Incorporate relevant keywords naturally into your listing's title and description. Think about what potential guests might search for, such as "cozy cabin near hiking trails" or "downtown apartment with city views." However, avoid keyword stuffing; the text should still be engaging and informative for the reader.

7. Highlight Unique Features and Experiences

Differentiate your listing by emphasizing what makes it unique. Whether it's a spectacular view, a pet-friendly policy, or proximity to local attractions, highlighting these features can make your listing more attractive to specific guest segments, improving your search ranking for those searches.

8. Engage with Your Reviews

Respond to reviews, both positive and negative, in a thoughtful and professional manner. This not only shows potential guests that you value feedback but also signals to Airbnb that you're an engaged and active host, which can positively influence your search ranking.

By implementing these strategies, you can significantly improve your Airbnb listing's search ranking. Remember, the goal is to align your hosting practices with Airbnb's mission of creating seamless and memorable guest experiences. As you refine your listing and operationalize these tips, you'll not only climb the search rankings but also build a thriving Airbnb business.

Chapter 3
Crafting the Perfect Listing

Chapter 3

Crafting the Perfect Listing

Welcome to the heart of your Airbnb success story—crafting the perfect listing. This chapter is dedicated to transforming your space into a compelling invitation that not only captures the essence of your offering but also stands out in a sea of options. With my background deeply rooted in digital and AI marketing, I've come to understand the power of presentation and the nuances of attracting an online audience. Here, I'll share with you the art and science behind creating an Airbnb listing that not only draws attention but also converts browsers into enthusiastic guests.

Creating the perfect listing is akin to telling a captivating story. It's about weaving together the unique attributes of your space with the expectations and desires of your potential guests. This process involves more than just listing amenities and providing a description. It's about creating a narrative that invites guests to imagine themselves in your space, experiencing the comfort, adventure, and tranquility you offer.

In this chapter, we'll explore the key components of a standout Airbnb listing, starting with the importance of high-quality, engaging photos that offer a visual tour of your space. We'll delve into the art of writing descriptions that tell a story, highlighting the features and experiences that make your listing unique. Attention will be given to the strategic use of titles and summaries that grab attention and convey your space's value proposition at a glance.

Moreover, we'll discuss how to effectively communicate the personality of your space and the surrounding area, creating a sense of place that resonates with your target audience. From showcasing local attractions to highlighting unique aspects of your property, this chapter will guide you in crafting a listing that not only stands out but also speaks directly to the interests and needs of your guests.

But crafting the perfect listing doesn't stop at visuals and narratives. We'll also cover the practical aspects of listing creation, such as setting the right price, understanding your competition, and optimizing your listing for search visibility. Each element of your listing, from the amenities you highlight to the house rules you set, plays a crucial role in attracting the right guests and setting the stage for a successful hosting experience.

As we embark on this journey of crafting the perfect listing, remember that the goal is to create a space that guests can't wait to experience. It's about more than just a transaction; it's about creating connections, memories, and experiences that last a lifetime. With the insights and strategies shared in this chapter, you'll be well on your way to creating an Airbnb listing that not only stands out but also becomes a sought-after destination for travelers from around the world.

Chapter 3-1

The best guidance on writing compelling titles and descriptions

In the digital marketplace of Airbnb, where countless listings vie for attention, the power of a compelling title and an engaging description cannot be overstated. These elements are not merely informational; they are your first—and often only—opportunity to make an impression on potential guests. I understand the nuances of crafting content that resonates. Here, I'll share insights into writing titles and descriptions that not only capture attention but also encapsulate the essence of your offering, compelling guests to explore further.

Crafting Compelling Titles

Your title is the headline of your listing, the hook that draws potential guests in. It should be concise yet descriptive, highlighting the most attractive and unique aspect of your space. Think of what sets your property apart—is it the breathtaking view, the cozy ambiance, or perhaps its prime location? Start with this feature, ensuring it's immediately clear why your listing is special.

- *Be Specific:* Vague titles get lost in the sea of listings. "Cozy Cabin with Mountain Views" is more enticing and informative than "Nice Cabin for Rent."

- *Use Adjectives Wisely:* Descriptive words add flavor to your title but use them judiciously to avoid sounding cliché. Choose adjectives that genuinely reflect the experience of staying at your place. *(I give you a couple of examples on page 25)*

- *Highlight Unique Features:* If your property has something truly unique, mention it in the title. "Historic Lighthouse with Panoramic Ocean Views" is bound to pique interest.

Writing Engaging Descriptions

Your description is where the story of your listing unfolds. This is your chance to elaborate on what makes your space unique, inviting guests to imagine themselves enjoying what you offer. A well-crafted description not only provides essential information but also evokes emotions and paints a vivid picture of the guest experience.

- **Start with a Bang:** Begin with the most compelling aspect of your property or offer. If your opening sentence grabs attention, potential guests are more likely to read on.

- **Create a Visual Journey:** Use descriptive language to guide potential guests through your space and the experiences it offers. Describe the comfort of the living area, the tranquility of the garden, or the gourmet possibilities in the kitchen.

- **Be Honest and Clear:** While it's important to highlight your space's best features, honesty about any limitations ensures guest satisfaction and avoids misunderstandings. Transparency builds trust.

- **Include Local Flavor:** Guests choose Airbnb for unique experiences. Mention nearby attractions, your favorite local café, or a hidden nature trail, offering guests a taste of what makes your location special.

- **Call to Action:** Conclude with an inviting call to action. Encourage potential guests to imagine themselves in your space, and suggest they book now to experience it for themselves.

Formatting for Readability:

- **Use Short Paragraphs:** Large blocks of text can be daunting. Break your description into short, digestible paragraphs.

- **Bullet Points for Amenities:** Highlight key amenities or features in bullet points for easy scanning.

- **Proofread:** Typos or grammatical errors can undermine the professionalism of your listing. A well-written, error-free description speaks volumes about the care you'll extend to your guests.

In crafting your title and description, remember that you're not just listing a space; you're offering an experience, a home away from home. By following these guidelines, you can create a compelling narrative that not only draws guests in but also turns the possibility of a stay into a promise of unforgettable memories.

Chapter 3-1

Titles examples

Certainly! Crafting a title for your Airbnb listing with the right balance of adjectives can significantly impact its appeal. Here are a few examples to illustrate how to use adjectives wisely:

Example 1: Before and After

- *Before:* "Nice Apartment in the City"
- *After:* "Charming Urban Retreat with Skyline Views"

In the "After" example, "Charming" and "Urban Retreat" offer a more vivid and enticing description than just "Nice," providing potential guests with a clearer sense of the atmosphere and experience. "Skyline Views" adds a specific and appealing detail that sets the listing apart.

Example 2: Before and After

- *Before:* "Good Location Near the Beach"
- *After:* "Serenene Beachside Haven Steps from the Sand"

Here, "Serene" and "Beachside Haven" evoke a more specific and inviting image than "Good Location," suggesting a peaceful and idyllic setting. "Steps from the Sand" gives a clear and attractive detail about the proximity to the beach.

Example 3: Before and After

- *Before:* "Big House with Garden"
- *After:* "Spacious Garden Oasis in Quiet Neighborhood"

"Spacious" is a more precise adjective than "Big," providing a sense of ample room without sounding exaggerated. "Garden Oasis" suggests not just a garden but a tranquil and beautiful outdoor space, and "in Quiet Neighborhood" adds context that might appeal to those seeking a peaceful stay.

Example 4: Before and After

- *Before:* "Modern Apartment with Amenities"
- *After:* "Sleek Designer Apartment with Rooftop Pool"

"Sleek" and "Designer" suggest a stylish and upscale experience, offering more intrigue than "Modern." Including a standout amenity like a "Rooftop Pool" in the title can significantly increase interest and set the listing apart from others.

Example 5: Before and After

- *Before:* "Cozy Cabin in the Mountains"
- *After:* "Enchanting Mountain Cabin with Woodland Views"

While "Cozy" is a positive descriptor, "Enchanting" adds a touch of magic and allure. "With Woodland Views" provides a picturesque detail, enhancing the appeal of a mountain stay.

These examples demonstrate how selecting the right adjectives and including specific details can transform a listing title from generic to captivating, drawing potential guests in with the promise of a unique and memorable experience.t

Chapter 3-2

The importance of honesty & transparency in your listing details

In the bustling world of Airbnb, where guests have countless options at their fingertips, the honesty and transparency of your listing details not only set the stage for guest expectations but also lay the foundation for trust and satisfaction. As a Central America traveler and a digital marketing expert, I've learned that the success of an Airbnb listing is deeply rooted in the authenticity of its presentation. This chapter underscores the critical importance of being honest and transparent in your Airbnb listing details, illustrating how this approach not only fosters positive guest experiences but also bolsters the longevity and reputation of your hosting business.

Building Trust with Potential Guests

Trust is the cornerstone of any successful Airbnb experience. From the moment potential guests encounter your listing, they're making decisions based on the information you provide. Accurate and transparent listing details help build trust from the outset, assuring guests that what they see is what they will get. This trust is crucial, as it influences not just their decision to book your property but also their attitudes and expectations upon arrival.

Setting Realistic Expectations

Honesty in your listing details helps set realistic expectations. By accurately describing your space, including its size, amenities, location, and any potential quirks or limitations, you allow guests to make informed decisions about whether your property meets their needs. This clarity helps prevent misunderstandings and disappointments, leading to more satisfied guests and, ultimately, positive reviews.

Avoiding Negative Reviews

One of the most direct consequences of misleading or inaccurate listing details is negative reviews. Guests who feel they were misled are not only likely to leave negative feedback but may also report your listing to Airbnb, potentially leading to penalties or removal from the platform. In contrast, honest and transparent listings, even if they reveal some less-than-ideal aspects of your property, set a clear expectation that can lead to more understanding and forgiving reviews.

Highlighting Unique Features and Managing Limitations

Transparency doesn't mean focusing solely on the negatives. It's also an opportunity to highlight what makes your property unique and appealing. Be open about your space's limitations, but also showcase its charm, character, and any unique features or amenities that set it apart. This balanced approach helps attract guests who are a good fit for your property, enhancing their overall experience.

Legal and Ethical Considerations

Beyond guest satisfaction, honesty and transparency in your listing are also matters of legal and ethical responsibility. Misrepresentation can lead to legal disputes and challenges, particularly if guests feel their safety or well-being was compromised by inaccurate listing information. Ethically, as hosts, we have a responsibility to ensure guests are fully informed about the space they're choosing to spend time in.

Long-term Benefits

In the long run, honesty and transparency in your Airbnb listing details contribute to a sustainable hosting business. They help you build a solid reputation as a trustworthy host, encourage repeat bookings, and foster positive word-of-mouth. In the competitive Airbnb market, your reputation can be one of your most valuable assets, attracting more guests and enabling you to command higher prices based on the quality and reliability of your offering.

In conclusion, the importance of honesty and transparency in your Airbnb listing details cannot be overstated. They are essential for building trust, setting realistic expectations, avoiding negative reviews, and ensuring legal and ethical compliance. By embracing honesty and transparency, you can enhance guest satisfaction, protect your reputation, and secure the long-term success of your Airbnb business. Remember, in the world of hospitality, trust and authenticity are your most precious commodities.

Chapter 4

Professional Photography Tips

Chapter 4

Professional Photography Tips

Welcome to Chapter 4, where we delve into the transformative power of professional photography in elevating your Airbnb listing. As a seasoned videographer and professional photographer, I have witnessed firsthand the profound impact that high-quality images can have on attracting potential guests and setting your listing apart in the competitive Airbnb marketplace. However, the essence of this chapter is to demystify the process and show you that capturing stunning photos of your rental doesn't require expert skills in Photoshop or expensive equipment.

Photography is not just about documenting a space; it's about storytelling. Through this lens, we'll explore how to use photography to convey the unique charm and comfort of your rental, creating an inviting visual narrative that resonates with viewers. The goal is to equip you with practical tips and techniques that can dramatically improve the appeal of your listing.

We'll start by covering the basics of good composition and lighting, two fundamental elements that can transform an ordinary photo into an extraordinary one. Understanding these principles will enable you to capture your space in the best possible light, highlighting its best features and creating an immediate emotional connection with potential guests.

Next, we'll discuss the importance of staging your space. A well-staged photograph not only looks professional but also helps guests envision themselves in your rental. From decluttering to adding small, personal touches, we'll go through simple yet effective staging techniques that can significantly enhance the visual appeal of your photos.

For those who may not have professional photography equipment, fear not. We'll explore how to make the most of the camera you already have, even if it's just your smartphone. With advancements in technology, smartphones are now capable of producing stunning high-quality images, and we'll delve into tips for leveraging these tools to their fullest potential.

Additionally, we'll touch on the basics of photo editing. While the thought of Photoshop might seem daunting, there are many user-friendly editing tools available that can help you enhance your photos without requiring extensive expertise. From adjusting brightness and contrast to cropping for the perfect composition, a few simple edits can make a world of difference in the final look of your images.

Chapter 4

n closing, remember that the essence of capturing great photos lies in showcasing the unique personality of your space and creating a welcoming atmosphere that guests can't resist. Whether you're a photography novice or have some experience behind the lens, this chapter will provide you with the knowledge and confidence to take captivating photos that will make your Airbnb listing shine.

Chapter 4-1

Why high-quality photos are crucial for your listing

In the visually driven world of online marketplaces, the imagery used to showcase your Airbnb listing plays a pivotal role in attracting potential guests. As both a videographer and a professional photographer, I, Mario L. Gagnon, have witnessed firsthand the transformative power of high-quality photography in capturing and conveying the essence of a space. However, it's essential to understand that you don't need to be an expert in Photoshop or own the most expensive camera equipment to achieve stunning results. The key lies in understanding the principles that make photos appealing and how they can significantly impact your listing's performance.

First Impressions Count

The first thing potential guests encounter when browsing Airbnb are photos. These images are not just pictures; they're your first opportunity to make an impression. High-quality photos instantly communicate value, care, and professionalism, setting the tone for what guests can expect. In contrast, poor-quality images can deter potential bookings, regardless of how exceptional your space might be.

Visual Storytelling

High-quality photos do more than show; they tell a story. They allow you to guide viewers through a visual journey of your space, highlighting unique features and creating an emotional connection. This visual storytelling is crucial in helping guests imagine themselves in your space, experiencing the comfort, beauty, and unique atmosphere you offer.

Competitive Edge

In a crowded marketplace, standing out is key. High-quality photos can give you a competitive edge, making your listing more memorable and appealing. They can showcase the best aspects of your property, from the cozy nooks to the sweeping views, in a way that words alone cannot convey. This visual appeal can be the deciding factor for guests choosing between your listing and another.

Chapter 4-1

Increased Engagement and Bookings

Statistics and studies consistently show that listings with high-quality photos receive more views, more saves, and ultimately, more bookings. Clear, well-composed, and well-lit photos can significantly increase your listing's visibility and attractiveness, leading to higher occupancy rates and potentially allowing you to command higher prices.

Trust and Transparency

High-quality photos also play a crucial role in building trust with potential guests. They provide a transparent and accurate representation of your space, reducing the risk of disappointment upon arrival. This transparency is vital for positive reviews and repeat bookings, as guests appreciate knowing exactly what to expect.

Achieving Professional-Quality Photos Without Being a Pro

While professional photography skills can undoubtedly enhance your listing's visual appeal, understanding the basics of good photography can also lead to impressive results. Key principles such as natural lighting, composition, and focusing on the details can dramatically improve the quality of your photos. Additionally, modern smartphones and affordable cameras are capable of capturing stunning images, especially when used thoughtfully.

In conclusion, high-quality photos are not just an optional extra for your Airbnb listing; they are an essential component of your marketing strategy. They have the power to attract, engage, and convince potential guests to book your space. By investing time and effort into capturing your property in the best light, you can significantly enhance your listing's performance, even without advanced photography skills or professional equipment. Remember, each photo tells a part of your story, and making that story as compelling as possible is key to your success on Airbnb.

Chapter 4-2
DIY photography tips for hosts

In the visually driven world of Airbnb, the quality of your listing's photos can significantly impact its success. While I bring my professional expertise as a videographer and photographer to the table, I understand that not every host has access to professional equipment or skills in Photoshop. Fortunately, capturing high-quality photos of your rental doesn't require you to be an expert. With a few DIY photography tips, you can produce compelling images that showcase the best of your space, attract more guests, and increase bookings. Here are some essential tips to help you capture your rental in the best light, quite literally.

1. Use Natural Light

Natural light is your best friend when it comes to photography. It can make your space look more inviting and spacious. Try to schedule your photo shoot during the day when sunlight is abundant but not too harsh, usually in the early morning or late afternoon. Open curtains and blinds to let in as much light as possible, and turn off most artificial lights to avoid mixed lighting conditions that can look unappealing in photos.

2. Understand Your Camera Settings

Whether you're using a DSLR, a compact camera, or a smartphone, familiarizing yourself with its settings can make a big difference. Most modern smartphones have advanced camera settings that allow for adjustments similar to those on professional cameras. Experiment with HDR (High Dynamic Range) mode to balance the light and dark areas of your photos, and use the grid feature to compose your shots using the rule of thirds for a more appealing composition.

3. Staging and Decluttering

Before you start snapping pictures, take the time to declutter and stage each room. Remove personal items and any clutter that doesn't contribute to the aesthetic appeal of your space. Staging involves arranging furniture and decor in a way that highlights the room's best features. Adding small touches, like a vase of fresh flowers or a neatly arranged set of towels, can make your space feel more welcoming and lived-in.

4. Focus on Unique Features

Every space has its unique features, whether it's a cozy fireplace, a panoramic view, or a quirky piece of art. Make sure to capture these elements, as they can make your listing stand out. Highlighting what makes your space unique can attract guests looking for an experience that matches their preferences.

5. Take Multiple Shots from Different Angles

Don't hesitate to take multiple shots of each room from various angles. This approach gives you a range of options to choose from and allows you to select the photos that best represent your space. Try shooting from corners to make rooms appear larger and from eye level to give a realistic perspective of the space.

6. Post-Processing

Basic post-processing can enhance your photos without requiring expert skills in Photoshop. Many free and user-friendly photo editing apps allow you to adjust brightness, contrast, saturation, and sharpness. Remember, the goal is to make your photos look as natural as possible, so avoid over-editing.

7. Consistency is Key:

Maintain a consistent look and feel across all your photos. This consistency helps create a cohesive and professional appearance for your listing. Use similar lighting conditions and editing styles for each photo to achieve a uniform look.

By following these DIY photography tips, you can create stunning visuals for your Airbnb listing that capture the essence of your space and appeal to potential guests. Remember, the goal is to present your rental in an honest and attractive light, showcasing the comfort, style, and unique features that make it a great place to stay.

Chapter 4-3

When to consider hiring a professional photographer

While DIY (Do it yourself) photography can significantly enhance your Airbnb listing, there are instances where investing in a professional photographer becomes not just beneficial but necessary. As someone deeply entrenched in the world of professional photography and videography, I can attest to the transformative power of expertly captured images. They not only elevate the presentation of your space but also communicate a level of professionalism and attention to detail that resonates with potential guests. Here, we explore the scenarios where hiring a professional photographer could be the key to unlocking the full potential of your Airbnb listing.

1. High Competition in Your Area

In regions where the Airbnb market is saturated, standing out becomes paramount. If your listing is one among hundreds of similar properties, professional photographs can give you a competitive edge. They can capture the unique essence and charm of your space in ways that amateur photos might not, making your listing more appealing to potential guests.

2. High-Value Properties

For hosts offering luxury accommodations or properties in high-demand locations, the stakes are inherently higher. Guests expecting a premium experience are more likely to be influenced by the quality of your listing's visuals. Professional photos that accurately reflect the quality and ambiance of your high-value property can justify higher price points and attract discerning guests.

3. Lack of Adequate Equipment or Skills

If you've attempted DIY photography and found that your equipment or skills aren't up to par, it might be time to call in a professional. Photographers not only come equipped with high-grade equipment but also possess the expertise to use lighting, angles, and composition to your advantage, ensuring your space is showcased at its absolute best.

4. Significant Investment in Renovations or Upgrades

If you've recently invested in upgrading or renovating your property, professional photographs can ensure that these improvements are highlighted effectively. Whether it's a brand-new kitchen, a landscaped garden, or upgraded amenities, a professional photographer can capture these features in a way that adds value to your listing and attracts more bookings.

5. When Your Listing Needs a Refresh

Over time, even the most successful Airbnb listings can benefit from a refresh. If you notice a decline in bookings or if your photos no longer reflect the current state of your property, new professional photos can breathe life into your listing. This is especially true if you've made significant changes to the decor or layout since your last photoshoot.

6. Maximizing Rental Income During Peak Seasons

For properties in areas with distinct high seasons, professional photos can help you capitalize on increased demand. High-quality images that showcase the best your property has to offer can make your listing more compelling, helping to ensure your space is booked out throughout these lucrative periods.

7. When Time Is of the Essence

Professional photographers can save you time and effort, especially if you're managing multiple properties or have a tight schedule. They can handle everything from staging to post-processing, delivering ready-to-upload images that meet your needs and exceed your expectations.

In conclusion, while DIY photography is a valuable skill for any Airbnb host, there are circumstances where the investment in a professional photographer can pay dividends. Whether it's standing out in a competitive market, highlighting a luxury property, or simply ensuring your listing is presented in the best possible light, professional photography can be a game-changer. Remember, in the world of online bookings, your photos are often the first and most impactful interaction potential guests have with your property. Making that interaction as positive as possible can significantly influence your Airbnb success.

Chapter 4-4

How to Take Great Airbnb Photos

Airbnb photos are your rental's visual handshake with potential guests, offering a snapshot of what they can expect from their stay. These images are pivotal in the decision-making process, often being the first element that catches a guest's eye when browsing through listings. When executed well, each photo serves as a compelling invitation, enhancing the allure of your listing and significantly boosting guest attraction. Recognizing the importance of photography in the Airbnb marketplace, it's crucial to understand that listings adorned with high-quality photos tend to secure more views and achieve higher placements in search results. Thus, mastering the art of Airbnb photography is not just an option but a necessity for hosts aiming to optimize their bookings.

Despite the critical role of photography, one doesn't need to be a professional photographer to capture the essence and appeal of their Airbnb property. With the right approach and a bit of know-how, anyone can produce stunning images that elevate their listing. This guide is designed to demystify the process, offering practical tips and insights to help you capture perfect Airbnb photos, even without professional expertise. From preparation to execution, we'll cover the essentials of Airbnb photography, ensuring you're equipped to showcase your rental in its best light.

Chapter 4-5

Optimal Number of Photos & Airbnb's Recommendations

While Airbnb allows up to 100 photos per listing, more is not always better. The key is to focus on quality over quantity. A selection of 20 to 30 well-composed, high-resolution images is ideal, providing a comprehensive view of your property without overwhelming potential guests. Each room should be represented by several carefully chosen photos, highlighting the space's best features.

Airbnb suggests adhering to a 3:2 width-to-length aspect ratio for photos, with a minimum resolution of 1024 x 683 pixels. This guideline ensures your images are optimized for display on the platform, offering a clear and appealing visual experience for viewers.

Chapter 4-6

Essential Equipment for Capturing Your Airbnb

The old adage, "a picture is worth a thousand words," rings especially true in the world of Airbnb listings. High-quality photos are the cornerstone of attracting guests, giving them a glimpse into your space and sparking their imagination. In this digital age, attention spans are short, and captivating photos are your first impression. But fear not, aspiring Superhost! You don't need a professional photographer's arsenal to achieve stunning results. Let's explore the tools that can elevate your Airbnb photography game:

For the Photography Enthusiast: Unleashing the Power of Your DSLR or Mirrorless Camera

If you own a DSLR or mirrorless camera, you have a powerful tool at your disposal. These cameras offer a level of control and flexibility that smartphones simply cannot match. Here's what to consider:

- Adjustable Settings: Aperture, shutter speed, and ISO are your creative playground. Mastering these settings allows you to control the depth of field, capture sharp images in low-light conditions, and achieve a variety of artistic effects.

Chapter 4-6

- Digital Format: Gone are the days of film! Embrace the digital revolution and shoot in RAW format whenever possible. RAW files capture a wider range of data compared to JPEGs, giving you more flexibility during editing for richer colors and sharper details.
- The Steadfast Tripod: Camera shake is the enemy of crisp photos. Invest in a sturdy tripod that will keep your camera perfectly still, especially when shooting in low-light or capturing wide-angle shots. A tripod allows you to experiment with slower shutter speeds, letting in more light for stunning nighttime or atmospheric interior shots.

Smartphones Can Shine Too: Utilizing Your Mobile Photography Companion
Smartphones are incredibly powerful tools, and their cameras have come a long way. While they may not offer the same level of control as DSLRs, you can still achieve fantastic results with a few key considerations:

- Embrace the Stand or Tripod: Even the steadiest hands can experience camera shake. Using a smartphone stand or a mini tripod ensures your photos are sharp and focused. Don't underestimate the power of a simple beanbag – its flexibility allows you to position your phone at unique angles for creative compositions.
- Lighting is Key: Natural light is your best friend. Open those curtains, schedule your photoshoot for a bright time of day, and position your space to maximize natural light. If artificial light is necessary, use multiple sources to avoid harsh shadows.
- Explore Smartphone Photography Apps: Many free and paid apps can enhance your smartphone photography experience. These apps offer features like manual controls, HDR (High Dynamic Range) for capturing detail in both shadows and highlights, and panorama modes for capturing expansive views.

Remember, the best camera is the one you have with you. Whether you're wielding a DSLR or using your smartphone, the most important thing is to experiment, have fun, and capture the unique personality and charm of your Airbnb space. In the next chapter, we'll delve into the art of composition and lighting, helping you transform your photos from snapshots to stunning showcases of your Airbnb haven.

Chapter 4-7

9 Helpful Hints for Perfect Airbnb Photography

1 - *Clean and Declutter:* A pristine, well-organized space is more inviting. Ensure your property is clean and free from clutter before photographing.

2 - *Prepare Each Room:* Attention to detail in room preparation can make a big difference. Open curtains to let in natural light, and add small touches like magazines or folded towels to enhance the space's appeal.

3 - *Optimal Lighting:* Utilize natural light for a professional look, and don't forget to turn on all indoor lights to eliminate shadows and highlight your property's features.

4 - *Shoot into a Corner:* This technique adds depth and makes rooms appear larger, offering a more inviting perspective.

5 - *Focus on Details:* Don't overlook the small, unique features of your property that can captivate potential guests.

Chapter 4-7

6 - *Panoramic Shots:* Use panoramic shots or a wide-angle lens to capture the full essence of each room, providing a comprehensive view of your space.

7 - *Diverse Angles:* Variety in photo angles keeps your listing interesting and engaging, allowing guests to envision themselves in your space.

8 - *Lifestyle Imagery:* Convey the lifestyle your property offers, using photos to suggest the experiences and comforts guests can enjoy.

9 - *Neighborhood Highlights:* Include images of the surrounding area, showcasing local attractions and the community vibe to entice guests further.

Chapter 5
Pricing Strategies for Maximum Profit

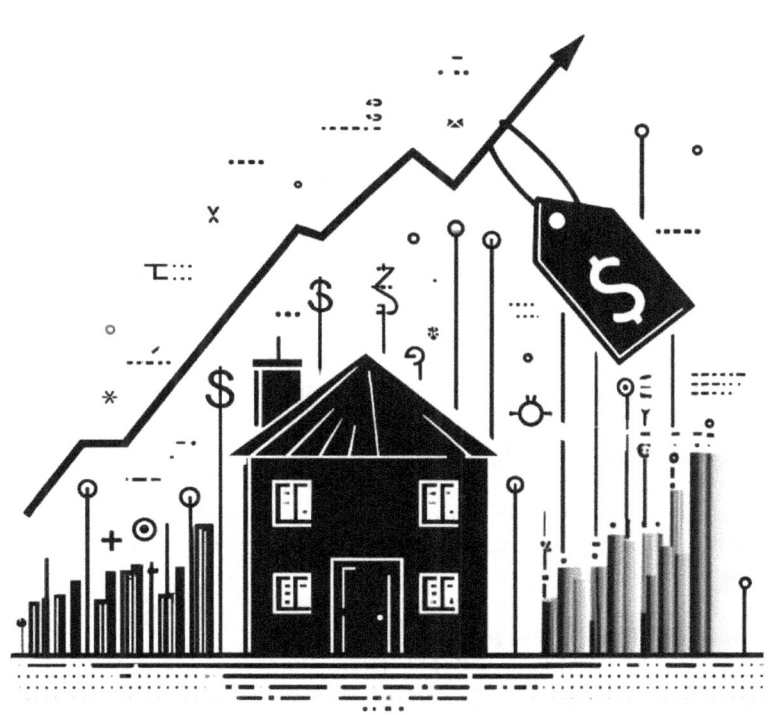

Chapter 5

Pricing Strategies for Maximum Profit

Navigating the competitive landscape of Airbnb hosting requires not just an appealing listing but also a strategic approach to pricing. In this crucial chapter, we delve into the art and science of pricing strategies that aim to maximize your profit while ensuring your property remains attractive to potential guests. As an expert in digital and AI marketing, and with extensive experience as a traveler and host, I, Mario L. Gagnon, understand the delicate balance between competitive pricing and profitability. Here, I will guide you through the intricacies of setting prices that not only reflect the value of your offering but also adapt to market dynamics, enhancing your occupancy rates and overall earnings.

Understanding Your Market

The foundation of any effective pricing strategy is a deep understanding of your local Airbnb market. This involves analyzing the demand patterns, seasonal fluctuations, and the pricing of comparable listings in your area. By grasitating these market dynamics, you can position your listing competitively, ensuring it appeals to the right audience at the right price.

Dynamic Pricing

One size does not fit all when it comes to pricing your Airbnb listing. Dynamic pricing involves adjusting your rates based on various factors, including demand, seasonality, and local events. This strategy ensures that your pricing is always optimized for maximum occupancy and profitability. Leveraging technology and data analytics can provide you with the insights needed to make informed pricing decisions, keeping you ahead in a constantly evolving market.

Psychological Pricing Techniques

The psychology behind pricing cannot be underestimated. Simple tactics, such as setting your price just below a round number (e.g., $99 instead of $100), can make your listing more appealing to potential guests. This chapter will explore various psychological pricing techniques and how they can be effectively applied to your Airbnb listing to enhance its attractiveness and boost bookings.

Chapter 5

Value Proposition

Your pricing strategy should also communicate the value guests will receive. This involves more than just the physical attributes of your property; it encompasses the entire guest experience, from the ease of booking to the quality of their stay. By clearly articulating the unique value proposition of your listing, you can justify your pricing and differentiate your offering in a crowded marketplace.

Promotions and Discounts

Strategically implemented promotions and discounts can serve as powerful tools to increase bookings during slow periods or to attract early bookings. Whether it's a last-minute discount, a reduced rate for longer stays, or a special offer for first-time guests, these incentives can drive occupancy without significantly undercutting your profitability.

Monitoring and Adjusting

A successful pricing strategy is not set in stone; it requires continuous monitoring and adjustment. Keeping an eye on your listing's performance, market trends, and guest feedback will allow you to tweak your pricing strategy as needed, ensuring it remains aligned with your goals and market conditions.

In this chapter, we will explore these aspects in detail, providing you with a comprehensive guide to developing and implementing a pricing strategy that maximizes your profit while maintaining a competitive edge. With the right approach, you can turn your Airbnb listing into a lucrative venture that stands out in a competitive market.

Chapter 5-1

Understanding your market & competitive pricing

In the dynamic world of Airbnb hosting, one of the keys to success lies in understanding your market and strategically setting competitive prices. This nuanced approach requires more than just a cursory glance at neighboring listings; it demands a deep dive into the intricacies of your local market, including demand fluctuations, seasonal trends, and the unique selling propositions of your property. As an expert in digital and AI marketing with a keen eye for detail honed through my experiences as a professional photographer and videographer, I, Mario L. Gagnon, will guide you through the process of mastering your market and leveraging competitive pricing to your advantage.

Market Research

The first step in understanding your market is thorough research. This involves analyzing not just the prices of similar listings in your area but also their occupancy rates, guest reviews, and the amenities they offer. Tools and platforms that aggregate Airbnb data can provide valuable insights into market trends, average nightly rates, and the factors that influence booking decisions in your locale. Pay attention to listings that consistently achieve high occupancy rates; these are your benchmarks for success.

Seasonal and Event-driven Demand

Your market's demand is not static; it fluctuates based on seasonality, local events, holidays, and even the day of the week. Identifying these patterns is crucial for setting prices that capitalize on high-demand periods while remaining attractive during slower times. For instance, if your property is in a city that hosts a major annual festival, you can adjust your prices to reflect the increased demand during that period. Similarly, understanding off-peak seasons allows you to adjust your strategy to maintain steady bookings year-round.

Chapter 5-1

Competitive Pricing Strategies

Setting competitive prices involves more than just undercutting the competition. It's about offering value that resonates with your target audience. This could mean pricing your listing slightly higher than average if you offer unique amenities or experiences that justify the premium. Conversely, if your goal is to increase occupancy during a slow season, a slight price reduction can make your listing more appealing without significantly impacting your profitability.

Dynamic Pricing Tools

Leveraging dynamic pricing tools can take the guesswork out of competitive pricing. These tools analyze vast amounts of data to recommend optimal pricing based on real-time market conditions, competitor pricing, and demand forecasts. By automating the pricing process, you can ensure your listing remains competitively priced at all times, maximizing your revenue potential.

The Importance of Reviews and Ratings

Your pricing strategy should also consider the intangible aspects of your listing, such as guest reviews and ratings. A property with stellar reviews can command higher prices because guests are willing to pay a premium for a proven, high-quality experience. Encourage satisfied guests to leave positive reviews and address any negative feedback promptly and professionally to maintain a strong online reputation.

Continuous Monitoring and Adjustment

Understanding your market and setting competitive prices is not a one-time task; it requires continuous monitoring and adjustment. Keep an eye on market trends, new listings, and changes in guest preferences. Regularly updating your pricing strategy in response to these factors ensures your listing remains competitive and profitable.

In conclusion, mastering your market and competitive pricing is an ongoing process that can significantly impact your success as an Airbnb host. By conducting thorough market research, understanding demand fluctuations, leveraging dynamic pricing tools, and maintaining a strong online reputation, you can develop a pricing strategy that maximizes both your occupancy rates and your overall profitability. Remember, in the competitive world of Airbnb hosting, knowledge is power, and staying informed is the key to staying ahead.

Chapter 5-2

Dynamic pricing tools & how to use them

In the dynamic world of Airbnb hosting, one of the keys to success lies in understanding your market and strategically setting competitive prices. This nuanced approach requires more than just a cursory glance at neighboring listings; it demands a deep dive into the intricacies of your local market, including demand fluctuations, seasonal trends, and the unique selling propositions of your property. As an expert in digital and AI marketing with a keen eye for detail honed through my experiences as a professional photographer and videographer, I, Mario L. Gagnon, will guide you through the process of mastering your market and leveraging competitive pricing to your advantage.

Market Research

The first step in understanding your market is thorough research. This involves analyzing not just the prices of similar listings in your area but also their occupancy rates, guest reviews, and the amenities they offer. Tools and platforms that aggregate Airbnb data can provide valuable insights into market trends, average nightly rates, and the factors that influence booking decisions in your locale. Pay attention to listings that consistently achieve high occupancy rates; these are your benchmarks for success.

Seasonal and Event-driven Demand

Your market's demand is not static; it fluctuates based on seasonality, local events, holidays, and even the day of the week. Identifying these patterns is crucial for setting prices that capitalize on high-demand periods while remaining attractive during slower times. For instance, if your property is in a city that hosts a major annual festival, you can adjust your prices to reflect the increased demand during that period. Similarly, understanding off-peak seasons allows you to adjust your strategy to maintain steady bookings year-round.

Competitive Pricing Strategies

Setting competitive prices involves more than just undercutting the competition. It's about offering value that resonates with your target audience. This could mean pricing your listing slightly higher than average if you offer unique amenities or experiences that justify the premium. Conversely, if your goal is to increase occupancy during a slow season, a slight price reduction can make your listing more appealing without significantly impacting your profitability.

Chapter 5-3

Seasonal pricing adjustments & special offers

In the dynamic world of Airbnb hosting, understanding and implementing seasonal pricing adjustments and special offers can significantly enhance your listing's appeal and profitability. The essence of a successful hosting strategy lies not only in presenting an attractive property but also in smart pricing that reflects the ebb and flow of demand throughout the year. As an experienced digital marketer and a seasoned traveler, I, Mario L. Gagnon, have seen firsthand the impact that well-thought-out pricing strategies can have on a listing's success. This section delves into the nuances of adjusting your pricing for seasonal trends and leveraging special offers to maximize occupancy and revenue.

Understanding Seasonal Demand

Seasonal demand varies widely depending on your property's location. Whether it's a beachfront villa that sees a surge in summer or a cozy mountain cabin popular in the winter, recognizing and anticipating these patterns is crucial. The first step is to analyze historical booking data for your area, noting peak seasons, shoulder seasons, and off-peak times. This understanding allows you to adjust your pricing strategy to match demand, ensuring you're not leaving money on the table during high-demand periods or struggling to attract guests during slower months.

Implementing Seasonal Pricing Adjustments

Once you've identified the seasonal trends affecting your listing, the next step is to adjust your pricing accordingly. During peak seasons, when demand is high, you can increase your rates to capitalize on the increased willingness of guests to pay for prime dates. Conversely, during off-peak times, consider lowering your prices to attract budget-conscious travelers. The key is to find the sweet spot where your pricing is competitive enough to drive bookings without undervaluing your offering.

Chapter 5-3

Leveraging Special Offers

Special offers are a powerful tool in your pricing strategy arsenal. They can be used to increase bookings during slow periods, encourage longer stays, or attract first-time guests. Some effective special offer strategies include:

- Last-minute discounts: Offer reduced rates for bookings made close to the check-in date to fill empty calendar slots.

- Early bird specials: Encourage bookings well in advance by offering discounts for reservations made several months ahead of time.

- Extended stay discounts: Provide lower per-night rates for guests who book longer stays, ensuring higher occupancy and reduced turnover costs.

Communicating Value

When implementing seasonal pricing adjustments and special offers, communication is key. Ensure that your listing clearly explains the value guests will receive by booking your property, whether it's a discounted rate for a week-long stay or the unique experience of visiting your location during a less crowded season. High-quality photos and descriptions that highlight seasonal attractions or amenities can also help justify your pricing and make special offers more enticing.

Monitoring and Adjusting

Effective seasonal pricing and special offer strategies require ongoing monitoring and flexibility. Keep an eye on your competitors, market trends, and booking patterns, adjusting your prices and offers as needed to stay competitive. Tools like dynamic pricing software can automate much of this process, but a hands-on approach ensures your strategy remains aligned with your goals and market realities.

In conclusion, mastering seasonal pricing adjustments and special offers can transform your Airbnb hosting experience. By strategically aligning your prices with market demand and leveraging offers to enhance your listing's appeal, you can maximize both occupancy and revenue throughout the year. Remember, the goal is to create a win-win situation where guests feel they're getting great value, and you're optimizing your earnings, regardless of the season.

Chapter 6
Enhancing Guest Experience

Chapter 6

Enhancing Guest Experience

In the bustling world of Airbnb hosting, where competition is fierce and guest expectations continue to rise, enhancing the guest experience has become more crucial than ever. This chapter delves into the art and science of creating memorable stays that not only meet but exceed guest expectations, turning first-time visitors into repeat guests and enthusiastic advocates for your listing. I've learned that the key to a successful Airbnb venture lies not just in attracting guests, but in making their stay unforgettable.

The guest experience encompasses every interaction from the initial booking inquiry to the moment they check out and even beyond. It's about creating a seamless, comfortable, and enriching stay that resonates on a personal level with each guest. This chapter will guide you through various strategies and insights aimed at elevating the guest experience, covering everything from the importance of clear and prompt communication to the thoughtful touches that make a space feel like home.

Communication is Key

Effective communication forms the backbone of an enhanced guest experience. This section will explore best practices for staying connected with your guests, providing timely and helpful information, and being responsive to their needs and inquiries. We'll discuss how to craft a welcome guide that not only introduces your guests to your home but also to the local area, offering them a curated experience.

Personalization Makes a Difference

In a market that values uniqueness, personalizing your guests' experiences can set your listing apart. We'll cover how to gather insights into your guests' preferences and tailor their stay accordingly, whether it's through custom recommendations, special amenities based on their interests, or even personalized welcome notes.

Chapter 6

The Little Things Count

Sometimes, it's the smallest details that leave the most significant impact. This section will delve into the myriad of ways you can add thoughtful touches to your space, from ensuring it's impeccably clean to providing those often-forgotten essentials that can make a guest's stay more comfortable and convenient.

Creating a Seamless Experience

From check-in to check-out, every aspect of your guests' stay should be as smooth and hassle-free as possible. We'll discuss the importance of a seamless check-in process, offering tips on using smart locks or lockboxes, and ensuring your house manual is clear and comprehensive.

Soliciting and Acting on Feedback

Feedback is a gift that allows you to continually improve the guest experience. This section will highlight the importance of soliciting feedback from your guests, responding gracefully to both praise and criticism, and making adjustments based on their suggestions.

Going Above and Beyond

Lastly, we'll explore how going the extra mile can turn a great stay into an extraordinary one. Whether it's through offering unexpected upgrades, providing insider tips on experiencing the locale like a local, or simply being available and attentive, we'll discuss how these efforts can significantly enhance guest satisfaction.

Enhancing the guest experience is an ongoing journey of learning and adaptation. By implementing the strategies outlined in this chapter, you can create a welcoming and memorable environment that not only delights your guests but also sets the foundation for a thriving Airbnb listing.

Chapter 6-1

Tips for creating a welcoming & memorable stay

Creating a welcoming and memorable stay for your Airbnb guests is an art that goes beyond mere accommodation. It's about crafting experiences that resonate, making guests feel valued and taken care of from the moment they step into your space until they depart. I've experienced firsthand the difference a thoughtful touch can make. Here, I share essential tips to elevate your hosting game, ensuring every guest leaves with lasting memories and a desire to return.

1. Personalized Welcome

Begin with a personalized welcome message, either sent digitally before arrival or placed prominently in the rental. Address your guests by name and express your excitement about hosting them. A small welcome gift, such as local snacks, a bottle of wine, or even a simple handwritten note, can set a warm and inviting tone for their stay.

2. Impeccable Cleanliness

Nothing says 'welcome' like stepping into a spotlessly clean space. Prioritize cleanliness and hygiene to make your guests feel comfortable and safe. Consider professional cleaning services for consistent standards and highlight your cleaning protocols in your listing to reassure guests.

3. Thoughtful Amenities

Stock your rental with amenities that cater to the comfort and convenience of your guests. Think beyond the basics; offer high-quality linens, plush towels, and a well-equipped kitchen. Small additions like a coffee maker with a selection of coffees and teas, fast and reliable Wi-Fi, streaming services, or a Bluetooth speaker can significantly enhance the guest experience.

4. Local Guidebook

Create a comprehensive guidebook that not only covers the house rules and how to use various appliances but also includes recommendations for local dining, shopping, attractions, and hidden gems. Personalize it with your favorite spots and insider tips to help guests experience the area like a local.

Chapter 6-1

5. Responsive Communication

Be readily available and responsive to your guests' needs and inquiries. Provide clear instructions for self-check-in and be flexible with check-in/check-out times when possible. Let them know they can reach out to you anytime, ensuring them that you're there to make their stay as enjoyable as possible.

6. Tailor Experiences

If you know your guests are visiting for a special occasion, such as an anniversary or birthday, consider tailoring their experience with a small gesture to celebrate the event. It could be as simple as leaving a congratulatory card or decorating a part of your space to acknowledge their celebration.

7. Comfort in Details

Pay attention to the details that contribute to overall comfort. Ensure your rental is well-stocked with essentials like toiletries, extra pillows, and blankets. Seasonal touches, such as providing warm throws in winter or beach towels and sunscreen in summer, can make a big difference.

8. Solicit Feedback

After their stay, reach out to guests to thank them for choosing your place and invite them to share their feedback. This not only shows that you value their opinion but also provides insights into how you can further improve the guest experience.

Creating a welcoming and memorable stay is about showing care and attention to your guests' needs and preferences. By implementing these tips, you can transform a good stay into an exceptional one, fostering a sense of belonging and connection that guests will remember long after they've departed. In the competitive world of Airbnb hosting, it's these personal touches and attention to detail that can set your listing apart and turn first-time guests into loyal returnees.

Chapter 6-2

The importance of amenities & personal touches

In the realm of Airbnb hosting, the amenities you offer and the personal touches you incorporate can significantly elevate the guest experience, setting your listing apart in a crowded marketplace. As a seasoned traveler, I have come to appreciate the profound impact that thoughtfully chosen amenities and personal touches can have on a guest's stay. They not only cater to the comfort and convenience of your guests but also reflect the care and attention you invest as a host. This chapter delves into the strategic selection of amenities and the integration of personal touches that can transform a standard stay into an unforgettable experience.

Amenities: Beyond the Basics

Amenities are the backbone of comfort in any Airbnb listing. While guests expect basic amenities such as clean bedding, towels, and Wi-Fi, going beyond these essentials can make a world of difference. Consider offering high-speed internet for business travelers, a fully equipped kitchen for families who prefer home-cooked meals, or a smart TV with access to streaming services for those rainy stay-in nights. Outdoor amenities like a grill, bicycles, or beach gear can enhance the appeal of your listing for guests looking to explore the outdoors. Remember, the goal is to anticipate the needs of your guests and cater to them proactively.

Personal Touches: Making It Memorable

Personal touches are what transform a stay from satisfactory to memorable. They are a reflection of your personality as a host and your dedication to creating a unique guest experience. Welcome baskets tailored to the occasion of the visit (such as local delicacies for foodies or a bottle of champagne for honeymooners) immediately make guests feel special. Customized guidebooks with your personal recommendations for dining, shopping, and local secrets invite guests to explore the area through your eyes.

Incorporating elements of local culture and art into your decor can also create a distinctive and immersive experience. Whether it's artwork from local artists, locally sourced furnishings, or books and magazines about the area, these touches not only beautify your space but also connect your guests with the local community.

Chapter 6-2

The Little Conveniences

It's often the smallest conveniences that leave the most significant impact on your guests. Think of amenities that address the "just in case" scenarios: umbrellas for unexpected rain, a sewing kit for minor repairs, or a first aid kit for minor mishaps. Providing chargers for various devices, a selection of teas and coffees, or even a pack of playing cards can add layers of comfort and convenience to your guests' stay.

Feedback and Evolution

Listening to your guests' feedback about amenities and personal touches is crucial for continuous improvement. Guests often appreciate the opportunity to suggest additions that could have made their stay even better. This feedback loop not only helps you refine your offerings but also demonstrates your commitment to guest satisfaction.

Conclusion

In conclusion, the amenities and personal touches you offer are not just about meeting the basic needs of your guests; they're about exceeding their expectations and creating a deeply personalized and memorable experience. By carefully selecting amenities that cater to the comfort and interests of your guests and adding personal touches that reflect thoughtfulness and care, you can elevate your Airbnb listing from a place to stay to a destination in its own right. Remember, in the competitive world of Airbnb hosting, it's these details that can make your property stand out and turn first-time guests into enthusiastic advocates and repeat visitors.

Chapter 6-3

Handling guest communications effectively

Effective communication is the cornerstone of a successful Airbnb hosting experience. It not only sets the tone for your guests' stay but also plays a crucial role in managing expectations, resolving issues, and ensuring a smooth and enjoyable experience for both parties. I've learned that the way hosts communicate can significantly impact their reputation and success on the platform. This chapter focuses on strategies for handling guest communications effectively, from the initial inquiry to post-checkout follow-up.

Prompt and Clear Responses

The importance of responding promptly to inquiries and messages cannot be overstated. A quick response time not only improves your chances of securing a booking but also sets a positive tone for the guest experience. Utilize Airbnb's messaging system to keep all communications in one place, ensuring nothing gets missed. Be clear and concise in your responses, and always aim to provide complete answers to guests' questions.

Personalization Goes a Long Way

While it's efficient to have templates for common responses, personalizing your communication can make guests feel valued and welcome. Use their name, reference specific details of their trip, and tailor your messages to their needs and inquiries. This personal touch can differentiate your hosting style and contribute to a memorable guest experience.

Setting Expectations

Clear communication is essential for setting and managing expectations. Be upfront about what guests can expect in terms of amenities, house rules, and any quirks or limitations of your property. Providing detailed information upfront can prevent misunderstandings and ensure guests are fully informed before their arrival.

Availability and Accessibility

Make it clear to your guests how and when they can reach you during their stay. Whether it's through the Airbnb app, phone, or another preferred method of communication, ensure guests feel comfortable reaching out with any questions or concerns. If you won't be available for a period, provide an alternative contact or make arrangements to ensure they have support if needed.

Proactive Communication

Don't wait for guests to reach out with problems or questions. Be proactive in your communication, checking in with them after their arrival to ensure everything is to their satisfaction and again midway through their stay. This not only demonstrates your commitment to their comfort but also provides an opportunity to address any issues before they escalate.

Handling Issues and Complaints

No matter how well you prepare, issues can arise. When they do, the manner in which you handle complaints and resolve problems can significantly impact your guests' overall satisfaction. Listen to their concerns, empathize with their situation, and take swift action to rectify the issue. Follow up to ensure they're happy with the resolution, showing that you value their feedback and are dedicated to improving their experience.

The Importance of Feedback

After guests check out, encourage them to leave a review of their stay. Constructive feedback is invaluable for identifying areas of improvement and enhancing future guests' experiences. Respond to reviews, both positive and negative, in a professional and grateful manner, demonstrating your appreciation for their input and your commitment to excellence.

In conclusion, effective guest communication is an art that requires attentiveness, empathy, and a proactive approach. By mastering this aspect of hosting, you can build strong relationships with your guests, leading to higher satisfaction rates, positive reviews, and ultimately, a more successful Airbnb listing. Remember, in the world of hospitality, communication is not just about exchanging information; it's about building connections and ensuring every guest feels heard, valued, and welcomed.

Chapter 7
Managing Reviews & Feedback

Chapter 7

Managing Reviews & Feedback

In the digital age, where decisions are often influenced by the experiences of others, managing reviews and feedback becomes a pivotal aspect of Airbnb hosting. This chapter delves into the nuanced art of navigating the waters of guest reviews, a domain where transparency, responsiveness, and improvement converge to shape your reputation and success on the platform. I've come to deeply appreciate the significant influence that adeptly handling reviews and feedback can exert on your Airbnb venture, especially through all my adventures in Airbnb properties across Central America.

Reviews are not just reflections of past stays; they are forward-looking indicators that potential guests rely on when choosing their next accommodation. Positive reviews can significantly enhance your listing's attractiveness, while negative feedback, if not managed properly, can deter future bookings. However, every review—good or bad—presents an opportunity for growth and improvement.

The Power of Positive Reviews

Positive reviews are the lifeblood of your Airbnb listing. They build trust, credibility, and desirability, serving as testimonials to the quality of your space and the excellence of your hosting. This chapter will guide you on how to encourage guests to leave positive feedback, highlighting the importance of creating memorable experiences that guests are eager to share.

Navigating Negative Feedback

Negative feedback, while challenging, is an invaluable source of insight. It offers a direct line to your guests' unmet expectations and areas where your offering could be enhanced. We will explore strategies for responding to and learning from negative reviews, turning potentially damaging feedback into a springboard for improvement and demonstrating your commitment to guest satisfaction.

Chapter 7

The Art of Response

Responding to reviews is as much an art as it is a necessity. Whether thanking a guest for glowing praise or addressing concerns raised in a less favorable review, your responses contribute to your public image. This chapter will provide best practices for crafting responses that are professional, empathetic, and constructive, reinforcing your reputation as a thoughtful and attentive host.

Leveraging Feedback for Improvement

Feedback, both positive and negative, is a goldmine of information that can guide your efforts to enhance your listing and the guest experience. We'll discuss how to analyze feedback trends, identify common themes, and implement changes that address your guests' needs and expectations, setting the stage for even better reviews in the future.

Encouraging Guest Reviews

Finally, we'll cover effective techniques for encouraging guests to leave reviews after their stay. From personalized thank-you messages to gentle reminders of the importance of reviews in the Airbnb community, this section will offer practical tips for increasing your review rate, thereby boosting your visibility and appeal on the platform.

In conclusion, managing reviews and feedback is a critical component of successful Airbnb hosting. It requires a proactive approach, a commitment to excellence, and a willingness to engage with and learn from your guests. By embracing reviews as opportunities for connection and growth, you can enhance your listing's reputation, attract more guests, and achieve greater success in the competitive world of Airbnb hosting.

Chapter 7-1

Strategies for encouraging positive reviews

In the competitive landscape of Airbnb hosting, positive reviews are not just accolades; they are essential tools for building trust, increasing visibility, and attracting future guests. Managing reviews from many types of clients, I have come to understand the critical role that positive feedback plays in the success of an Airbnb listing. Encouraging guests to leave positive reviews requires a blend of exceptional hospitality, strategic communication, and a genuine commitment to guest satisfaction. This chapter outlines effective strategies to maximize the likelihood of receiving positive reviews, thereby enhancing your listing's appeal and driving your Airbnb business forward.

Deliver an Exceptional Guest Experience

The foundation of positive reviews is an exceptional guest experience. From the cleanliness of your space to the comfort of the bed, every detail contributes to the overall impression of your guests. Go above and beyond to ensure your property not only meets but exceeds guest expectations. Personal touches, such as a welcome note or a small gift, can make a significant impact. Remember, guests are more likely to leave a review when their stay is memorable for all the right reasons.

Clear and Open Communication

Effective communication is key to a positive Airbnb experience. From the moment a booking is made, keep the lines of communication open and clear. Provide guests with all the information they need about your space and be available to answer questions promptly. After check-in, reach out to ensure everything is to their satisfaction. This proactive approach not only helps in resolving any issues that may arise but also demonstrates your commitment to their comfort, making them more inclined to leave a positive review.

Personalize the Guest Experience

Personalization can significantly enhance the guest experience, making your space feel more like a home than a rental. Tailor your interactions based on the information guests share about their visit. Whether it's recommending a local restaurant for an anniversary dinner or providing toys for guests with children, these personalized touches can leave a lasting impression and inspire positive reviews.

Chapter 7-1

Simplify the Review Process

Make it easy for guests to leave a review by guiding them through the process. After their stay, send a personalized thank-you message expressing your appreciation for their visit and gently remind them to leave a review. You can also mention how valuable their feedback is to you as a host and to the wider Airbnb community. Simplifying this process by providing clear instructions can significantly increase your chances of receiving feedback.

Respond to All Reviews

Responding to reviews, both positive and negative, shows future guests that you value feedback and are actively engaged in providing a great experience. Thank guests for their positive comments and, if there are criticisms, address them constructively and professionally. This not only demonstrates your commitment to improvement but also can turn a negative review into a positive showcase of your responsiveness as a host.

Encourage Feedback During the Stay

Encourage guests to share their feedback during their stay. This not only allows you to address any issues in real-time, ensuring their experience is as positive as possible but also increases the likelihood of receiving a positive review at the end of their stay. Let guests know that you're available to make their stay more comfortable and that their satisfaction is your top priority.

In conclusion, encouraging positive reviews is an art that requires attention to detail, proactive communication, and a genuine desire to provide an outstanding guest experience. By implementing these strategies, you can increase the number of positive reviews your listing receives, which in turn can enhance your reputation on Airbnb, attract more guests, and ultimately contribute to the success of your hosting business. Remember, each positive review is a stepping stone towards building a thriving Airbnb presence.

Chapter 7-2

How to respond to reviews, both positive and negative

In the world of Airbnb hosting, reviews are more than just feedback; they are a public record of your commitment to guest satisfaction and an opportunity to showcase your hospitality skills. I understand the importance of responding to reviews in a manner that enhances your reputation and appeals to potential guests. This section provides a comprehensive guide on how to craft thoughtful responses to both positive and negative reviews, turning each piece of feedback into an opportunity for growth and improved guest relations.

Responding to Positive Reviews

Positive reviews are a cause for celebration and an opportunity to reinforce your brand's positive aspects. When responding:

1. Express Gratitude: Always start by thanking the guest for choosing your place and for taking the time to leave a review. A simple expression of gratitude can go a long way in making guests feel appreciated.

2. Personalize Your Response: Mention specific details the guest appreciated about their stay or any personal interactions you had. This personal touch shows future guests that you are attentive and engaged.

3. Invite Them Back: Encourage satisfied guests to return. A gentle invitation not only fosters repeat business but also signals to potential guests that you're confident in the quality of your offering.

4. Highlight Improvements: If a guest mentions something they particularly enjoyed, use this as an opportunity to highlight recent upgrades or related amenities that future guests can look forward to.

Responding to Negative Reviews

Negative reviews, while challenging, are invaluable for learning and improvement. Your response should be prompt, professional, and constructive.

1. Stay Calm and Professional: Approach each negative review without defensiveness. Acknowledge the guest's feedback in a calm and professional manner, showing that you take their concerns seriously.

2. Apologize and Empathize: Offer a sincere apology for any aspects of their stay that did not meet expectations. Empathy demonstrates that you value guest satisfaction and are committed to making things right.

3. Offer a Solution: Whenever possible, explain how you've addressed or plan to address the issues raised. This not only reassures the reviewer but also signals to potential guests that you are proactive about resolving problems.

4. Take the Conversation Offline: For complex issues, invite the guest to continue the conversation privately. This allows for a more personalized resolution and prevents the airing of grievances in a public forum.

5. Highlight Positive Changes: If the feedback has led to positive changes, mention this in your response. It shows that you're responsive to feedback and committed to continuous improvement.

6. Keep It Brief: While it's important to address specific points, avoid overly lengthy responses that can become defensive or dilute your message. Aim for concise, constructive replies.

General Tips for All Responses:

Be Timely: Respond to reviews as quickly as possible. Timeliness shows that you're attentive and engaged with your guests' feedback.

Maintain Your Brand Voice: Ensure your responses reflect the personality and professionalism of your Airbnb brand. Consistency helps build trust with potential guests.

Use Reviews as a Learning Tool: Beyond responding, take the time to reflect on the feedback provided. Reviews are a valuable resource for understanding guest expectations and identifying areas for improvement.

In conclusion, effectively responding to reviews is a critical aspect of managing your Airbnb listing. Whether celebrating positive feedback or addressing criticisms, each response is an opportunity to showcase your commitment to excellence in hospitality. By adopting a thoughtful, professional, and constructive approach to review responses, you can enhance your reputation, encourage repeat business, and attract new guests to your property.

Chapter 7-3

Using feedback to improve your listing & guest experience

In the dynamic world of Airbnb hosting, feedback is not just a measure of past performance but a blueprint for future success. Grasping the subtleties of what truly satisfies guests, I've come to realize the critical importance of feedback in improving both your listing and the entire guest experience. In this section, I'll share how to effectively utilize feedback, transforming insights into tangible improvements and taking your hosting to the next level. It's essential to acknowledge and act upon this to ensure continuous enhancement and success.

Embrace All Feedback

The first step in leveraging feedback is to embrace it in all its forms. Positive feedback confirms what you're doing right and should be replicated or enhanced. Negative feedback, while initially disheartening, is a goldmine of opportunities for improvement. It highlights areas that may not align with guest expectations and provides a clear direction for making impactful changes.

Analyze Feedback for Patterns

One-off comments can be insightful, but the real power of feedback lies in identifying patterns. Regularly review your reviews and messages to spot recurring themes. Are guests consistently commenting on the comfort of the beds, or are there frequent mentions of a particular amenity missing? Recognizing these patterns helps prioritize the changes that will have the most significant impact on guest satisfaction.

Implement Changes Based on Feedback

Once you've identified areas for improvement, it's time to implement changes. This could range from upgrading your Wi-Fi speed to addressing a commonly noted inconvenience. When you make a change based on guest feedback, consider communicating this in your listing description or in responses to reviews. This not only shows prospective guests that you're responsive and committed to improvement but also invites past guests to return and experience the enhancements.

Chapter 7-3

Communicate Improvements to Future Guests

After implementing changes, make sure to update your listing and communicate these improvements in your interactions with potential guests. Highlighting that you've made specific upgrades based on guest feedback can significantly enhance your listing's appeal. It demonstrates your dedication to providing the best possible experience and can be a deciding factor for guests choosing between multiple listings.

Use Feedback to Enhance Personalization

Feedback can also provide insights into the preferences and expectations of your target audience, allowing you to tailor the guest experience more closely to their desires. For example, if you notice a trend of families staying at your property, you might consider adding family-friendly amenities or creating a guide to local kid-friendly attractions.

Foster an Ongoing Feedback Loop

Encourage guests to share their experiences and suggestions during and after their stay. Make it easy for them to provide feedback by sending a follow-up message thanking them for their stay and asking for any comments or recommendations. An ongoing feedback loop not only aids in continuous improvement but also builds a relationship with guests, making them feel valued and heard.

Celebrate the Positive, Learn from the Negative

Finally, it's essential to maintain perspective. Celebrate the positive feedback as a testament to your efforts and view negative feedback as a learning opportunity. Both are integral to your growth and success as a host. Responding to feedback, whether through a thank-you message or by making tangible changes, shows that you value your guests' input and are committed to excellence.

In conclusion, feedback is a powerful tool in the Airbnb hosting arsenal. By actively seeking, analyzing, and acting on guest feedback, you can make informed decisions that enhance your listing and elevate the guest experience. This proactive approach to improvement not only leads to better reviews and increased bookings but also fosters a sense of fulfillment in providing exceptional hospitality. Remember, in the journey of hosting, feedback is the compass that guides you toward becoming a standout Airbnb host.

Chapter 8

Marketing Your Airbnb

Chapter 8

Marketing Your Airbnb

In the bustling world of short-term rentals, having a beautiful and well-maintained property is just the beginning. The key to maximizing occupancy and ensuring your Airbnb stands out from the competition lies in effective marketing. This chapter delves into the multifaceted approach to marketing your Airbnb, drawing from my extensive background in digital and AI marketing. I've navigated the complexities of online visibility and guest engagement, and I'm here to share insights that will elevate your listing from just another option to a sought-after destination!

Marketing your Airbnb involves a strategic blend of online presence, social media engagement, and leveraging the power of word-of-mouth. It's about telling the story of your space and the experiences it offers, reaching potential guests where they are most attentive, and creating compelling reasons for them to book your property over others. In this chapter, we will explore actionable strategies to enhance your Airbnb's market appeal, increase its visibility, and attract more guests.

Building a Strong Online Presence

Your Airbnb listing is the cornerstone of your online presence, but it shouldn't be the only place where potential guests can find you. We'll discuss how to create a comprehensive online profile for your property, including setting up a dedicated website, engaging with potential guests on social media platforms, and listing your property on multiple rental platforms to maximize visibility.

Utilizing Social Media Effectively

Social media is a powerful tool for connecting with potential guests and showcasing the unique aspects of your Airbnb. From sharing stunning photos on Instagram to providing updates and special offers on Facebook, we'll cover how to use these platforms to create a buzz around your property and engage with a broader audience.

Leveraging Reviews and Testimonials

Positive reviews and testimonials are invaluable in convincing potential guests to book your property. We'll explore strategies for encouraging guests to share their experiences and how to leverage these reviews across your marketing channels to build trust and credibility.

Chapter 8

Creating Compelling Content

Content marketing can significantly enhance your property's appeal. Whether it's blog posts about local attractions, videos showcasing your property, or newsletters offering special promotions, creating compelling content can attract more guests. We'll provide tips on content creation that resonates with your target audience and drives bookings.

Engaging with Local Businesses and Events

Collaborating with local businesses and tapping into local events can provide mutual benefits and increase your property's visibility. From offering package deals with local tour operators to promoting local festivals and events, we'll discuss how to integrate your Airbnb into the local community and tourism landscape.

Measuring and Adjusting Your Strategies

Finally, we'll cover the importance of measuring the effectiveness of your marketing efforts and making necessary adjustments. By analyzing booking data, website traffic, and social media engagement, you can refine your marketing strategies to better target potential guests and increase occupancy rates.

Marketing your Airbnb is an ongoing process that requires creativity, adaptability, and a keen understanding of your target market. With the right approach, you can turn your property into a thriving short-term rental business that stands out in a crowded market. Let's embark on this journey to unlock the full potential of your Airbnb through strategic marketing.

Chapter 8-1

Beyond the platform: Marketing your listing on social media & other channels

In today's digital age, the success of your Airbnb listing is significantly influenced by your ability to market it beyond the confines of the Airbnb platform itself. Drawing from my experience as a marketing expert, I've seen the remarkable impact that utilizing social media and digital platforms can have on increasing visibility and securing more bookings. This chapter will delve into the numerous strategies available to broaden the exposure of your Airbnb listing, establishing an engaging online presence that draws in potential guests from across the digital landscape.

Establishing a Social Media Presence

Social media platforms like Instagram, Facebook, and Pinterest offer unique opportunities to showcase your property and engage with a broader audience.

- Instagram is ideal for sharing high-quality images and stories of your property, offering a visual tour that highlights its best features and the experiences guests can enjoy. Utilize hashtags related to travel, your location, and Airbnb to increase visibility.

- Facebook allows for more extensive interaction through the creation of a dedicated page for your listing. Here, you can share updates, special offers, and reviews. Engaging with local community groups can also drive interest.

- Pinterest is perfect for showcasing your property through themed boards, such as "Dreamy Getaways" or "City Escapes," and linking back to your Airbnb listing or personal website.

Creating a Dedicated Website

A dedicated website for your Airbnb property provides a centralized platform where potential guests can find detailed information, stunning galleries, guest testimonials, and direct booking options. It also enhances your property's professional image and can improve search engine visibility. Incorporate SEO (Search Engine Optimization) strategies to ensure your website ranks well for relevant search queries.

Chapter 8-1
Email Marketing

Building an email list of past guests and interested prospects allows you to keep in touch and encourage repeat bookings. Send out newsletters with updates about your property, information on local events, and exclusive offers. Personalization is key; tailor your messages to reflect the preferences and interests of your audience.

Collaborations and Partnerships

Partnering with local businesses, influencers, and tourism boards can amplify your marketing efforts. Collaborations can range from offering package deals with local attractions to hosting social media influencers in exchange for coverage. These partnerships not only increase your listing's exposure but also enhance the guest experience by providing added value.

Utilizing Online Travel Agencies and Niche Platforms

While Airbnb is a dominant player in the vacation rental market, listing your property on additional platforms like VRBO, Booking.com, and niche sites that cater to specific types of travelers can expand your reach. Each platform attracts a different audience, increasing your chances of bookings throughout the year.

Content Marketing

Creating engaging content that highlights the unique aspects of your property and its surroundings can attract potential guests. Blog posts, videos, and online guides that offer insider tips on enjoying the local area not only provide value to readers but also drive traffic to your listing. Share this content across your social media channels and website to engage a wider audience.

Measuring Success and Adjusting Strategies

Finally, it's crucial to monitor the performance of your marketing efforts across all channels. Use analytics tools to track website traffic, social media engagement, and conversion rates. This data will help you understand what's working and where there's room for improvement, allowing you to refine your strategies for even better results.

In conclusion, marketing your Airbnb listing beyond the platform requires a multifaceted approach that leverages the strengths of social media, digital marketing, and community engagement. By creating a compelling online presence and engaging with potential guests across various channels, you can significantly increase the visibility of your listing, attract more bookings, and build a successful Airbnb business.

Chapter 8-2

Building a brand for your Airbnb rental

In the competitive landscape of Airbnb rentals, establishing a strong, recognizable brand for your property can be the difference between blending in and standing out. Over the past 20 years, working with a diverse range of clients has shown me the undeniable influence of branding in turning properties into highly desired destinations. A meticulously developed brand does more than just encapsulate the spirit of your rental; it effectively conveys its distinct appeal to prospective guests. In this chapter, I'll lead you through the journey of crafting a compelling brand for your Airbnb rental, making certain it connects with your intended audience and creates an enduring impact.

Define Your Unique Selling Proposition (USP)

The first step in building your brand is to identify what makes your rental unique. Is it the breathtaking view, the impeccable design, the unbeatable location, or perhaps the exceptional service you provide? Your USP is what sets you apart from the competition and should be the cornerstone of your branding efforts.

Create a Cohesive Visual Identity

A strong visual identity is crucial for brand recognition. This includes a consistent color scheme, typography, and a logo that reflects the personality of your rental. These elements should be used consistently across all your marketing materials, from your Airbnb listing to your social media profiles and your own website. High-quality, visually appealing photos are also a key component of your visual identity, showcasing your property in the best light.

Develop a Compelling Brand Message

Your brand message is the narrative that ties together the unique aspects of your rental and communicates them to your audience. It should encapsulate the experience guests can expect when they stay at your property. Whether it's relaxation and tranquility, adventure and exploration, or luxury and indulgence, your brand message should be clear, compelling, and consistently conveyed in all your communications.

Chapter 8-2

Leverage Social Media to Tell Your Story

Social media platforms are powerful tools for storytelling and brand building. Use them to share the story behind your rental, highlight guest experiences, and showcase the lifestyle your property offers. Engaging content, such as behind-the-scenes looks, local tips, and updates on new features or amenities, can help build a community around your brand and engage potential guests.

Offer Consistent, Exceptional Service

At the heart of your brand should be a commitment to providing exceptional service. This includes everything from the cleanliness of your space and the quality of amenities to the responsiveness of your communication and the personal touches that make each stay special. Consistent, positive guest experiences reinforce your brand promise and lead to positive reviews, which are invaluable for brand credibility.

Encourage Word-of-Mouth and Leverage User-Generated Content

Happy guests are your best brand ambassadors. Encourage them to share their experiences on social media and review sites, and make it easy for them to tag your property or use a specific hashtag. User-generated content not only provides social proof but also contributes to the authenticity and relatability of your brand.

Monitor and Adapt Your Brand Strategy

Building a brand is an ongoing process. Regularly monitor how your brand is perceived by guests and the broader market. Solicit feedback, keep an eye on trends, and be willing to adapt your strategy as needed to ensure your brand remains relevant and appealing to your target audience.

In conclusion, building a brand for your Airbnb rental involves a strategic blend of defining your unique value, creating a cohesive visual identity, crafting a compelling message, and delivering exceptional service. By establishing a strong brand, you can differentiate your property in a crowded marketplace, attract more guests, and create a memorable experience that keeps them coming back. Remember, your brand is more than just a logo or a color scheme; it's the entire experience you offer to your guests.

Chapter 8-3

Partnering Locally to Elevate Guest Experiences

In the quest to create an unforgettable Airbnb experience, collaboration with local businesses and attractions can play a pivotal role. Such partnerships not only enrich the guest experience but also embed your rental into the fabric of the local community, offering guests an authentic taste of the area. Drawing on my past experiences, where I facilitated numerous partnerships with local businesses to boost my clients' ventures through strategic associations — a tactic that proved highly effective — I've come to understand the significant impact of tapping into local networks to enhance the guest experience. This chapter delves into the power of collaboration with local businesses and attractions, showcasing how such partnerships can turn your Airbnb listing into a gateway to the distinct culture, cuisine, and activities of your area.

Identifying Potential Partnerships

Start by identifying local businesses and attractions that align with your brand and can enhance your guests' stay. These could include cafes, restaurants, tour operators, museums, and even local artisans. The goal is to curate a list of partners that offer experiences which resonate with your guests' interests and your property's unique selling proposition.

Building Mutually Beneficial Relationships

Approach potential partners with a proposal that outlines the benefits of collaboration for both parties. For local businesses, your Airbnb can provide a steady stream of customers, while they offer your guests unique experiences or discounts. It's a symbiotic relationship that enhances the value proposition for both your listing and the local business.

Creating Exclusive Offers for Your Guests

Work with your partners to create exclusive offers or packages for your guests. This could be a discount at a popular local restaurant, a private tour of a nearby attraction, or a custom experience crafted just for your guests. These exclusive offers not only make your guests feel valued but also encourage them to explore the local area, contributing to the local economy.

Chapter 8-3

Integrating Local Experiences into Your Listing

Once you've established partnerships, integrate these local experiences into your Airbnb listing. Highlight the unique local attractions and the exclusive offers available to your guests in your property description and welcome guide. This not only adds value to your listing but also helps set it apart from competitors.

Leveraging Social Media and Online Content

Use your social media platforms and any online content you create to promote your local partnerships. Share stories or posts about the local experiences guests can enjoy when staying at your property. This not only markets your Airbnb but also promotes your local partners, fostering a sense of community and collaboration.

Gathering Feedback and Refining Offerings

After guests have taken advantage of these local experiences, solicit their feedback. This will help you gauge the value these partnerships add to your guests' stay and identify areas for improvement. Use this feedback to refine your offerings and strengthen your partnerships.

Contributing to the Local Community

Collaborating with local businesses and attractions not only enhances your guests' experience but also contributes to the local community's economy and vitality. It's a way to ensure that your Airbnb business benefits not just you and your guests but also the area where your property is located.

In conclusion, collaborating with local businesses and attractions is a strategic approach to enhancing the guest experience, offering visitors unique insights and access to the local culture and community. These partnerships can significantly differentiate your Airbnb listing, making it more attractive to potential guests and increasing their satisfaction during their stay. By integrating local experiences into your Airbnb offering, you create a win-win-win situation for your guests, your partners, and your business, fostering a sense of community and connection that resonates with travelers seeking authentic experiences.

Chapter 9

Legal Considerations & Best Practices

Chapter 9

Legal Considerations & Best Practices

Navigating the legal landscape of Airbnb hosting is as crucial as creating an inviting space for guests. This chapter delves into the essential legal considerations and best practices that every host needs to be aware of to ensure a smooth, compliant, and successful hosting experience. Drawing from my own journey through the intricacies of local regulations, insurance policies, and community standards, I aim to equip you with the knowledge and tools necessary to operate your Airbnb with confidence and integrity.

The realm of short-term rentals is governed by a complex web of laws and regulations that can vary significantly from one location to another. Understanding these legal requirements is not just about compliance; it's about fostering a responsible and sustainable hosting environment that respects the rights and expectations of all stakeholders involved, including guests, neighbors, and local communities.

Local Regulations and Zoning Laws

One of the first steps in legal compliance is understanding the specific regulations and zoning laws that apply to short-term rentals in your area. This section will guide you through navigating local government websites, consulting with legal professionals, and leveraging resources provided by Airbnb to understand the

legal framework governing your rental. Whether it's obtaining the necessary permits, adhering to safety and health standards, or understanding tax obligations, being well-informed is your first line of defense against potential legal challenges.

Insurance and Liability

Insurance is a critical aspect of hosting, providing protection for both you and your guests. We'll explore the types of insurance policies available, including Airbnb's Host Protection Insurance, and how they apply to different scenarios you might encounter as a host. Understanding the extent of your coverage and any gaps is essential for mitigating risks and ensuring peace of mind.

Chapter 9
Understanding and Drafting House Rules

Clear and comprehensive house rules are not just guidelines for guest behavior; they are also a legal tool that helps protect your property and ensure the safety and comfort of all parties. This section will offer insights into drafting effective house rules that are both fair and enforceable, covering everything from noise restrictions to pet policies.

Privacy Considerations

In the digital age, privacy concerns are paramount. We'll discuss best practices for respecting your guests' privacy, including the legal implications of security cameras and data protection. Ensuring guests feel safe and their privacy is respected is not just a legal requirement but a cornerstone of trust and hospitality.

Navigating Neighbor Relations

Maintaining good relationships with your neighbors is crucial for a harmonious community and the long-term success of your Airbnb. We'll cover strategies for engaging with neighbors, addressing their concerns, and preventing disputes before they escalate into legal issues.

Staying Updated on Legal Changes

Laws and regulations governing short-term rentals are constantly evolving. This section will provide tips on staying informed about legal changes that could affect your hosting business, including subscribing to local government newsletters, joining host communities, and participating in local meetings.

Implementing Best Practices

Finally, this chapter will synthesize legal considerations into actionable best practices that you can implement to ensure your hosting operation is not only compliant but also exemplary. From record-keeping and reporting to ethical hosting and community engagement, adopting these best practices will set you apart as a responsible and respected host.

In conclusion, understanding and adhering to the legal considerations and best practices of Airbnb hosting is fundamental to building a sustainable and successful rental business. By taking a proactive approach to compliance, insurance, privacy, and community relations, you can create a hosting environment that is safe, respectful, and welcoming for everyone involved. Armed with the right knowledge and tools, you're well on your way to navigating the legal landscape of Airbnb hosting with confidence.

Chapter 9-1

Navigating local regulations & Airbnb policies

Navigating the maze of local regulations and Airbnb policies is a critical aspect of becoming a successful and responsible Airbnb host. The landscape of short-term rental laws can be complex, varying significantly from one jurisdiction to another, and understanding these rules is essential to operate legally and avoid potential fines or legal issues. Additionally, Airbnb's own policies provide a framework for what is expected from hosts in terms of safety, hospitality, and respect for the community. This chapter aims to equip you with the knowledge and strategies to navigate these regulations and policies effectively, ensuring your hosting journey is both compliant and rewarding.

Understanding Local Regulations

Local regulations on short-term rentals can include zoning laws, licensing requirements, occupancy taxes, and restrictions on the number of days a property can be rented out. The first step in compliance is to thoroughly research the specific regulations applicable in your area. This may involve visiting local government websites, attending city council meetings, or consulting with a legal professional who specializes in real estate or short-term rental laws. It's also wise to connect with other local hosts, as they can offer insights based on their own experiences with compliance.

Securing Necessary Permits and Licenses

Many municipalities require hosts to obtain permits or licenses to operate a short-term rental. The application process can vary, but it typically involves submitting detailed information about your property, paying a fee, and sometimes undergoing a property inspection. Keep meticulous records of all your interactions with local authorities and any permits or licenses you obtain, as you may need to provide proof of compliance to Airbnb or in the event of a dispute.

Chapter 9-1

Airbnb Policies and Community Standards

In addition to local laws, Airbnb hosts must adhere to the platform's policies and community standards, which are designed to ensure safety, reliability, and respect within the Airbnb community. These policies cover a wide range of topics, from listing accuracy and safety standards to anti-discrimination policies and rules for interacting with guests. Familiarize yourself with these policies by reviewing the resources provided on Airbnb's website and staying updated on any changes, as Airbnb frequently updates its policies to respond to new challenges and feedback from the community.

Handling Occupancy Taxes

Many jurisdictions require the collection and remittance of occupancy taxes for short-term rentals. Airbnb offers a feature in some locations where it automatically collects and remits these taxes on behalf of hosts. However, in areas where this service is not available, it's your responsibility to understand the tax requirements, collect the appropriate taxes from guests, and remit them to the local tax authority. This may require registering with the tax authority and filing regular tax returns.

Insurance and Liability

Ensuring you have adequate insurance coverage is another crucial aspect of compliance. While Airbnb provides a Host Protection Insurance program, it's important to review this coverage and determine if additional insurance is needed to cover potential gaps. This might include property damage insurance or additional liability coverage, especially if your property has unique features like a pool or hot tub.

Staying Informed and Proactive

Laws and policies regarding short-term rentals are continually evolving. Stay informed about changes in your local regulations and Airbnb policies by subscribing to relevant newsletters, joining host forums, and participating in community meetings. Being proactive about compliance can prevent legal issues and contribute to a positive reputation as a host.

In conclusion, navigating local regulations and Airbnb policies is a foundational element of responsible hosting. By taking the time to understand and comply with these requirements, you can ensure your Airbnb operates within legal boundaries, providing a safe and welcoming environment for your guests. Remember, compliance is not just about following the rules; it's about contributing to the sustainability and positive growth of the short-term rental ecosystem..

Chapter 9-2

Insurance & safety tips for hosts

For Airbnb hosts, ensuring the safety of your property and guests is paramount, not just for the well-being of those staying but also for the longevity and success of your hosting business. Equally important is having the right insurance coverage to protect against potential liabilities. This chapter delves into essential insurance considerations and safety tips for hosts, aiming to provide a comprehensive guide to safeguarding your property, your guests, and yourself from unforeseen events.

Understanding Insurance Needs

Airbnb provides a Host Protection Insurance program, which offers liability coverage to hosts and landlords worldwide, at no additional cost. This program protects against third-party claims of property damage or bodily injury up to $1 million. However, it's crucial to understand the limitations of this coverage and assess whether additional insurance is necessary for your specific situation.

Many hosts will find it beneficial to carry a separate short-term rental insurance policy that covers risks not included in Airbnb's Host Protection Insurance. This can include property damage caused by guests, loss of income due to unforeseen property damage making your space unrentable, and more comprehensive liability coverage.

Regularly Review and Update Your Insurance Policy

The insurance landscape is continually evolving, especially as short-term rentals become more prevalent. Regularly review your policy to ensure it still meets your needs and make updates as your hosting situation changes. This might include increasing coverage limits or adding new policies as you expand your hosting business.

Implementing Safety Measures

Safety is a critical concern for guests and should be a top priority for any host. Start by conducting a thorough safety audit of your property. Identify potential hazards and take steps to mitigate them. This can include installing smoke and carbon monoxide detectors, securing rugs and railings, and ensuring that all appliances are in good working order.

Provide clear safety information for your guests. This includes emergency contact numbers, the location of first aid kits, fire extinguishers, and instructions for emergency procedures. Make sure this information is easily accessible in your welcome book and posted in a prominent location within your property.

Securing Your Property

While making your property safe for guests, it's also important to secure it against unauthorized access or burglary. Invest in quality locks for all doors and windows, and consider smart locks or keyless entry systems that allow you to change access codes between guests. Security cameras and alarm systems can also deter unauthorized entry, but be sure to respect your guests' privacy and comply with local laws regarding surveillance.

Regular Maintenance Checks

Preventative maintenance is key to avoiding accidents and ensuring your property remains in top condition. Regularly check for and repair any potential hazards, such as loose handrails, leaky pipes, or electrical issues. Keeping your property well-maintained not only reduces the risk of accidents but also contributes to positive guest reviews.

Educating Guests on Safety Practices

Educate your guests on how to safely use the features and amenities of your property. This includes instructions for appliances, hot tubs, fireplaces, and any other equipment that could pose a risk if misused. Providing clear, written instructions can help prevent accidents and ensure guests have a safe and enjoyable stay.

Conclusion

Insurance and safety are intertwined aspects of hosting that require careful consideration and proactive management. By securing the right insurance coverage and implementing comprehensive safety measures, you can protect your guests, your property, and your hosting business. Remember, a safe and secure property is not just a legal and financial safeguard; it's a cornerstone of the exceptional hospitality that guests will remember and appreciate.

Chapter 9-3

Ethical hosting practices

Ethical hosting practices are the backbone of a sustainable and responsible Airbnb business. They not only ensure compliance with legal standards but also foster a positive environment for guests, the local community, and the host. Ethical hosting encompasses a range of practices, from fair pricing and transparency to respecting the rights and dignity of guests and neighbors. As a host, I've come to understand that the success of my Airbnb listing is deeply intertwined with my commitment to these principles. This chapter aims to guide you through the essential ethical practices that can enhance your hosting experience, contribute to a positive reputation, and ensure the long-term viability of your rental business.

Transparency and Honesty

Transparency is fundamental to ethical hosting. This means being honest and clear about what guests can expect from their stay. Accurately describe your listing, including any potential limitations or quirks of your property. Misleading guests, whether intentionally or not, can lead to disappointment, negative reviews, and even disputes. Always provide a truthful representation of your space, amenities, and the surrounding area.

Fair Pricing

Setting fair and transparent pricing is another cornerstone of ethical hosting. Avoid exploiting high-demand periods by excessively raising prices beyond what is reasonable for your listing's value and the local market. While dynamic pricing strategies are common and acceptable, they should be applied in a way that remains fair to guests. Additionally, be upfront about any additional fees, such as cleaning fees or extra guest charges, so guests know exactly what to expect.

Respecting Guest Privacy

Respecting the privacy of your guests is paramount. This includes not only physical privacy within the rental space but also data privacy. Be cautious about how you collect, use, and store personal information. If you use security cameras or other monitoring devices for security purposes, fully disclose their presence and location to your guests in advance, ensuring you comply with Airbnb's policies and local laws regarding surveillance.

Chapter 9-3

Promoting Inclusivity and Non-discrimination

Airbnb's community is built on the principle of inclusivity. As a host, it's essential to adhere to Airbnb's non-discrimination policy, welcoming guests regardless of race, religion, nationality, gender, sexual orientation, age, or disability. Ethical hosting means creating a space where all guests feel safe, respected, and valued.

Engaging with the Local Community

Ethical hosting also involves being a good neighbor and actively engaging with your local community. This includes adhering to noise ordinances, managing guest behavior, and ensuring your Airbnb does not disrupt the local quality of life. Participate in community meetings and stay informed about local concerns and issues related to short-term rentals. By fostering positive relationships with your neighbors, you contribute to the community's well-being and sustainability.

Environmental Responsibility

Incorporating sustainable practices into your hosting can significantly reduce your environmental impact. Simple measures like providing recycling bins, using energy-efficient appliances, and encouraging guests to conserve water can make a big difference. Ethical hosting involves considering the broader impact of your rental activity and taking steps to mitigate negative effects on the environment.

Continuous Improvement

Finally, ethical hosting is an ongoing commitment to improvement. Solicit feedback from your guests and neighbors, and be open to making changes based on their suggestions. Stay informed about best practices in hospitality and sustainability, and continually look for ways to enhance your hosting practices.

In conclusion, ethical hosting practices are not just about adhering to rules and regulations; they're about fostering a positive, inclusive, and sustainable hosting environment. By committing to transparency, fairness, privacy, inclusivity, community engagement, environmental responsibility, and continuous improvement, you can build a reputable and successful Airbnb business that benefits guests, the community, and yourself.

Chapter 10

Scaling Your Airbnb Business

Chapter 10

Scaling Your Airbnb Business

Expanding your Airbnb business is a journey that moves beyond the initial success of hosting a single property. It's about leveraging your experience, insights, and the reputation you've built to grow your presence on the platform and increase your earnings. This chapter is dedicated to guiding you through the process of scaling your Airbnb business, from adding new listings to optimizing operations and enhancing guest experiences across multiple properties. As someone who has navigated the complexities of the Airbnb market, I've learned that scaling requires a strategic approach, focusing on efficiency, quality, and sustainability.

Strategic Expansion

The decision to expand your Airbnb business should be driven by careful consideration and strategic planning. This includes market research to identify lucrative opportunities, understanding the financial implications of acquiring or leasing additional properties, and ensuring you can maintain the high standards of hospitality that contributed to your initial success. We'll explore how to assess potential markets, select properties that align with your brand, and calculate the investment needed to grow your portfolio.

Operational Efficiency

Scaling your Airbnb business introduces new challenges in managing multiple listings. Operational efficiency becomes crucial. This section will cover the tools and systems you can implement to streamline your operations, from automated booking and communication systems to cleaning and maintenance workflows. Emphasizing efficiency in your operations ensures you can maintain quality and responsiveness as your business grows.

Building a Team

As your Airbnb business expands, so too does the need for support. Building a reliable team is essential for sustaining growth. This might include property managers, cleaners, and maintenance personnel. We'll discuss how to build, manage, and motivate a team that shares your commitment to excellence in hospitality, ensuring that each property is managed to your standards.

Chapter 10

Maintaining Quality Across Listings

Consistency in quality across all your properties is key to scaling successfully. This involves not only maintaining the physical standards of your properties but also ensuring that the guest experience is uniformly excellent. We'll delve into strategies for quality control, guest communication, and personal touches that can make each of your listings stand out.

Leveraging Technology

Technology plays a pivotal role in efficiently managing multiple Airbnb listings. From property management software to guest experience platforms, we'll explore the technological tools that can help you scale your operations, enhance guest satisfaction, and optimize your pricing strategy across multiple properties.

Marketing and Branding

As you scale, your brand becomes even more important. A strong, cohesive brand across all your listings can help attract guests and build loyalty. This section will cover advanced marketing and branding strategies, including building a dedicated website, engaging with guests through social media, and creating a memorable brand experience that encourages repeat bookings and referrals.

Sustainability and Community Engagement

Finally, scaling your Airbnb business responsibly involves considering the impact on local communities and the environment. We'll discuss how to grow sustainably, ensuring that your expansion contributes positively to the communities where you operate and adheres to ethical hosting practices.

In conclusion, scaling your Airbnb business is an exciting opportunity to build upon your success and increase your impact in the world of hospitality. By approaching expansion with strategic planning, operational efficiency, a focus on quality, and a commitment to sustainability, you can create a thriving Airbnb portfolio that delights guests and stands the test of time.

Chapter 10-1

Expanding your portfolio with additional properties

Expanding your Airbnb portfolio by adding additional properties is a significant milestone in the journey of any host. It represents not just growth in terms of quantity but also an opportunity to diversify your offerings and increase your revenue streams. However, expansion comes with its own set of challenges and considerations. Strategic planning, market research, and financial analysis become even more critical as you scale up. This chapter aims to guide you through the process of expanding your portfolio, ensuring that each new property not only contributes to your business's growth but also aligns with your vision and values as a host.

Market Research and Selection

The first step in expanding your portfolio is conducting thorough market research. This involves identifying locations with high demand for short-term rentals, understanding the competitive landscape, and analyzing market trends. Look for areas that complement your existing property or properties, offering guests different experiences—be it a city break, a beach getaway, or a country retreat. Consider factors such as seasonality, local attractions, and accessibility, which can significantly impact your occupancy rates and pricing strategy.

Financial Planning and Investment Analysis

Expanding your portfolio requires substantial financial investment. It's crucial to conduct a detailed financial analysis to assess the viability of adding new properties. This includes calculating the initial investment needed for purchasing or leasing and renovating properties, ongoing operational costs, and potential revenue. Consider different financing options, such as mortgages, loans, or partnerships, and evaluate their implications on your business's cash flow and profitability. Setting clear financial goals and benchmarks will help you monitor the performance of your new properties and make informed decisions about further expansion.

Operational Scalability

As you add more properties to your portfolio, the complexity of managing your Airbnb business increases. Developing scalable operational systems is essential for maintaining efficiency and ensuring a high-quality guest experience across all listings. This might involve investing in property management software, automating guest communication, and streamlining check-in and check-out processes. Consider whether to manage properties directly or hire property managers, especially if the new properties are in different locations.

Building and Managing a Team

Scaling your Airbnb business often requires building a team to handle different aspects of the operation, from cleaning and maintenance to guest services and administration. Hiring the right people and establishing clear roles and responsibilities are key to ensuring smooth operations. Invest in training your team to maintain the standards of hospitality that define your brand, and foster a culture of excellence and continuous improvement.

Maintaining Quality and Consistency

As your portfolio grows, maintaining consistent quality across all properties becomes a challenge. Implement regular quality checks and gather guest feedback to ensure that every property meets your standards. Consistency in the design, amenities, and guest experience can help strengthen your brand and encourage guests to explore your other properties.

Legal and Regulatory Compliance

Navigating the legal and regulatory landscape is increasingly complex with a multi-property portfolio. Ensure compliance with local zoning laws, licensing requirements, and tax obligations for each property. Staying informed about changes in regulations and adapting your practices accordingly is crucial to avoid legal issues and fines.

Marketing and Branding

Effectively marketing your expanded portfolio is crucial for attracting guests to your new properties. Develop a cohesive branding and marketing strategy that highlights the unique features of each property while reinforcing the overall brand identity of your Airbnb business. Utilize a mix of channels, including social media, email marketing, and partnerships with local businesses, to reach a wider audience.

In conclusion, expanding your Airbnb portfolio with additional properties is an exciting opportunity to grow your business and diversify your offerings. By carefully selecting new properties, planning your finances, scaling your operations, and maintaining high standards of quality and compliance, you can successfully manage a multi-property portfolio that delights guests and contributes to your long-term success as a host.

Chapter 10-2

Outsourcing and automating tasks for efficiency

As your Airbnb business grows, the demands on your time and resources increase exponentially. Managing multiple properties requires a significant amount of work, from guest communication and booking management to cleaning and maintenance. To maintain high standards of hospitality while also scaling your business, it becomes essential to look for ways to increase efficiency. Outsourcing and automating tasks are two strategies that can help you manage your workload more effectively, allowing you to focus on strategic aspects of your business and ensuring a consistent guest experience across all your properties.

The Power of Automation

In the digital age, automation has become a game-changer for Airbnb hosts. Leveraging technology to automate repetitive tasks can save you time, reduce errors, and enhance guest satisfaction. Here are some areas where automation can make a significant impact:

- *Booking and Communication:* Automated messaging systems can handle initial guest inquiries, booking confirmations, check-in instructions, and follow-up messages. Personalizing these communications while automating their delivery ensures guests receive timely information without requiring your constant attention.

- *Pricing Strategy:* Dynamic pricing tools adjust your rental rates in real-time based on market demand, competition, and other factors. Automating your pricing strategy helps ensure your listings are competitively priced to maximize occupancy and revenue.

- *Guest Screening:* Implementing automated screening criteria for guests can help you manage who books your property, reducing the risk of problematic stays. Automation tools can check guests against your specified criteria, such as past reviews or verification status, streamlining the booking process.

Chapter 10-2

Outsourcing for Scalability

While automation can handle many operational aspects of your Airbnb business, personal touch and on-the-ground tasks still require human intervention. Outsourcing these tasks to professionals can free up your time and ensure high-quality service for your guests. Consider outsourcing the following:

- *Cleaning and Maintenance:* Professional cleaning services ensure your properties are spotless and well-maintained, meeting guests' expectations. Regular maintenance checks by professionals can also prevent minor issues from becoming major problems.

- *Property Management:* If managing day-to-day operations becomes too time-consuming, hiring a property management company can be a wise investment. They can handle guest communications, bookings, cleaning, and maintenance, allowing you to focus on strategic growth.

- *Virtual Assistants:* For administrative tasks such as managing bookings across platforms, updating calendars, or handling guest inquiries, a virtual assistant can be invaluable. They can manage these tasks remotely, providing support without the need for a full-time employee.

Implementing Systems and Processes

Whether you're automating tasks or outsourcing them, having clear systems and processes in place is crucial. Document all operational procedures, from guest check-in and check-out processes to emergency protocols. This ensures that everyone involved in managing your properties, be it software or a service provider, is on the same page and can deliver consistent service.

Monitoring and Quality Control

Even with tasks automated or outsourced, maintaining oversight is essential to ensure standards are met. Regularly review performance metrics, guest feedback, and the quality of work done by your service providers. This allows you to make informed adjustments to your operations, ensuring your business runs smoothly and your guests are satisfied.

In conclusion, outsourcing and automating tasks are key strategies for scaling your Airbnb business efficiently. By leveraging technology and professional services, you can streamline operations, maintain high standards of guest experience, and focus on strategic aspects of growth. Remember, the goal is not just to expand your portfolio but to do so in a way that is sustainable, manageable, and aligned with the exceptional service that defines your brand.

Chapter 10-3

Long-term strategies for success in the Airbnb market

Achieving sustained success in the Airbnb market requires more than just short-term tactics and operational efficiency. It demands a strategic approach that encompasses understanding market dynamics, building a strong brand, fostering guest loyalty, and staying adaptable to changes in the industry. As a host who has navigated the ebbs and flows of the Airbnb ecosystem, I've learned that long-term success is built on a foundation of quality, consistency, and strategic foresight. This chapter explores the key strategies that can help you secure a prosperous future in the competitive world of Airbnb hosting.

Deep Market Understanding

A profound understanding of the Airbnb market and its trends is crucial for long-term success. This involves continuously monitoring market conditions, guest preferences, and competitive offerings in your area. Stay informed about global travel trends, economic factors affecting tourism, and technological advancements in the hospitality industry. Use this knowledge to anticipate shifts in demand, adjust your offerings, and position your properties to appeal to emerging guest segments.

Building a Strong Brand

In a marketplace crowded with options, a strong, recognizable brand can set your listings apart and drive guest loyalty. Your brand should reflect the unique qualities of your properties and the exceptional experiences you offer. Invest in professional branding, including a memorable logo, a cohesive visual identity, and a compelling brand story. Consistently convey your brand message across all platforms, from your Airbnb listings to your social media channels and website, to build recognition and trust with guests.

Fostering Guest Loyalty

Repeat guests are a testament to the quality of your hosting and a reliable source of revenue. Foster guest loyalty by delivering consistently outstanding experiences, personalizing guest interactions, and showing appreciation for their business. Implement a guest loyalty program, offering incentives such as discounts on future stays or special perks for repeat bookings. Engage with past guests through email marketing, sharing updates about your properties and exclusive offers to encourage them to book again.

Chapter 10-3

Adapting to Technological Advances

The Airbnb market is continually shaped by technological advances, from the rise of smart home technology to the use of artificial intelligence in guest service. Embrace these technologies to enhance the guest experience, streamline operations, and stay competitive. For example, smart locks can facilitate seamless check-ins, while AI-powered chatbots can provide instant assistance to guests. Keeping abreast of technological trends and incorporating relevant innovations into your properties can significantly enhance your appeal in the market.

Sustainability Practices

Sustainability is becoming increasingly important to travelers, with many guests seeking eco-friendly accommodation options. Implementing sustainable practices in your properties not only contributes to environmental conservation but also enhances your market appeal. This can include energy-efficient appliances, water-saving fixtures, recycling programs, and the use of eco-friendly cleaning products. Highlighting your commitment to sustainability in your listings can attract a growing segment of eco-conscious guests.

Community Engagement and Social Responsibility

Engaging with the local community and practicing social responsibility can enrich the guest experience and bolster your reputation. Partner with local businesses, participate in community events, and support local causes. This not only strengthens your network and contributes to the local economy but also offers guests an authentic connection to the community. Demonstrating a commitment to social responsibility can also differentiate your brand in a competitive market.

Continuous Learning and Improvement

The Airbnb market is dynamic, with guest preferences and industry standards constantly evolving. Commit to continuous learning and improvement, seeking feedback from guests, staying informed about industry best practices, and regularly evaluating and updating your properties and services. This mindset of growth and adaptation is key to maintaining relevance and achieving long-term success in the Airbnb market.

Conclusion: Mastering the Art of Airbnb Hosting

As we reach the conclusion of this comprehensive journey through the multifaceted world of Airbnb hosting, it's clear that success on this platform is both an art and a science. From crafting the perfect listing and creating memorable guest experiences to navigating legal considerations and scaling your business, each chapter has provided insights and strategies designed to elevate your hosting game. The journey of an Airbnb host is one of continuous learning, adaptation, and commitment to excellence.

The essence of Airbnb hosting lies not just in providing a place to stay but in offering experiences that resonate, connections that last, and spaces that feel like home. Whether you're just starting out with a single property or looking to expand your portfolio, the principles outlined in this book aim to guide you towards creating meaningful and sustainable success in the Airbnb market.

Embrace the Journey

Remember, the path to becoming a successful Airbnb host is a journey, not a destination. It's a journey marked by constant evolution, challenges to overcome, and opportunities to grow. Embrace each step of this journey with an open mind and a willingness to adapt. The landscape of short-term rentals is ever-changing, influenced by market trends, technological advancements, and shifting guest expectations. Staying informed, flexible, and responsive to these changes is crucial.

Build on Foundations of Hospitality

At the heart of your Airbnb business should always be the foundational principles of hospitality: respect, care, and a desire to provide outstanding experiences. These principles are timeless and universal, transcending market fluctuations and trends. By building your hosting practices on these foundations, you can ensure that your business not only survives but thrives in the long term.

Foster Connections

Airbnb hosting offers a unique opportunity to connect with people from all walks of life, sharing cultures, stories, and experiences. These connections are what often transform a good stay into an unforgettable one. Foster these connections with your guests, your community, and fellow hosts. They enrich your hosting experience and contribute to a sense of fulfillment that extends beyond financial success.

Commit to Continuous Improvement

The pursuit of excellence in Airbnb hosting is an ongoing process of refinement and improvement. Solicit feedback from your guests, reflect on your experiences, and always look for ways to enhance your offerings. Whether it's upgrading your amenities, implementing new technologies, or exploring innovative marketing strategies, there's always room for growth.

Look to the Future

As you move forward in your Airbnb hosting journey, keep an eye on the horizon. The future of short-term rentals is bright, filled with potential for hosts who are prepared to innovate, adapt, and lead. Whether your goals include expanding your portfolio, increasing your profitability, or simply creating more memorable experiences for your guests, the future is yours to shape.

In closing, the journey of mastering the art of Airbnb hosting is as rewarding as it is challenging. It's a journey that demands dedication, creativity, and a genuine passion for hospitality. Armed with the insights and strategies from this book, you are well-equipped to navigate the complexities of Airbnb hosting and achieve success on your terms. Here's to your journey, your growth, and the endless possibilities that await you in the world of Airbnb hosting.

www.ingramcontent.com/pod-product-compliance
Lightning Source LLC
Chambersburg PA
CBHW050326230526
45471CB00005B/2372